REA's Books Are The Best...
They have rescued lots of grades and more!

(a sample of the <u>hundreds of letters</u> REA receives each year)

"Your books are great! They are very helpful, and have upped my grade in every class. Thank you for such a great product."
Student, Seattle, WA

"Your book has really helped me sharpen my skills and improve my weak areas. Definitely will buy more."
Student, Buffalo, NY

"Compared to the other books that my fellow students had, your book was the most useful in helping me get a great score."
Student, North Hollywood, CA

"I really appreciate the help from your excellent book. Please keep up your great work."
Student, Albuquerque, NM

"Your book was such a better value and was so much more complete than anything your competition has produced (and I have them all)!"
Teacher, Virginia Beach, VA

(more on next page)

(continued from previous page)

" Your books have saved my GPA, and quite possibly my sanity. My course grade is now an 'A', and I couldn't be happier. "

Student, Winchester, IN

" These books are the best review books on the market. They are fantastic! "

Student, New Orleans, LA

" Your book was responsible for my success on the exam. . . I will look for REA the next time I need help. "

Student, Chesterfield, MO

" I think it is the greatest study guide I have ever used! "

Student, Anchorage, AK

" I encourage others to buy REA because of their superiority. Please continue to produce the best quality books on the market. "

Student, San Jose, CA

" Just a short note to say thanks for the great support your book gave me in helping me pass the test . . . I'm on my way to a B.S. degree because of you ! "

Student, Orlando, FL

COLLEGE & UNIVERSITY WRITING

By Robert Blake Truscott
Douglass/Cook College Writing Center
Rutgers University
New Brunswick, New Jersey

And the Staff of
Research & Education Association
Dr. M. Fogiel, Director

Research & Education Association
61 Ethel Road West
Piscataway, New Jersey 08854

SUPER REVIEW®
OF COLLEGE & UNIVERSITY WRITING

Year 2003 Printing

Printed in the United States of America

Library of Congress Control Number 00-130283

International Standard Book Number 0-87891-185-5

WHAT THIS Super Review WILL DO FOR YOU

This **Super Review** provides all that you need to know to do your homework effectively and succeed on exams and quizzes.

The book focuses on the core aspects of the subject, and helps you to grasp the important elements quickly and easily.

Outstanding **Super Review** features:

- Topics are covered in logical sequence

- Topics are reviewed in a concise and comprehensive manner

- The material is presented in student-friendly language that makes it easy to follow and understand

- Individual topics can be easily located

- Provides excellent preparation for midterms, finals and in-between quizzes

- In every chapter, reviews of individual topics are accompanied by Questions **Q** and Answers **A** that show how to work out specific problems

- At the end of most chapters, quizzes with answers are included to enable you to practice and test yourself to pinpoint your strengths and weaknesses

- Written by professionals and test experts who function as your very own tutors

Dr. Max Fogiel
Program Director

CONTENTS

CHAPTER **1**

Introduction to College and University Writing

1.1 What Professors Want

Whether you're attending a two- or four-year college, professors have the same expectations: that you will graduate with (a) the skills to write critically about, and respond analytically to, literature and issues of the day and (b) the ability to compose standard business documents—letters, reports, and proposals. The need for writing spans the full gamut of academic courses. History and geology majors alike must come to terms with writing the research paper, not only in their chosen field but also in a basic English composition course.

Most professors will insist that students control not only the basic format, grammar, organization, logic, and punctuation of the writing submitted, but also learn to use the English language with skill and accuracy. Knowing the basic vocabulary of English and the specialized vocabulary of a chosen discipline is essential to success, just as in a job it is essential to be able to produce cogent documents on a timely basis. Your professors want you to leave college able to handle the typical tasks of writing in life, to enjoy writing and reading in English, and to be an effective critical thinker.

1.2 The Curriculum of College and University Writing

As we've said, the need to write essays and reports cuts across all disciplines. In general, your professors will require you to respond to environmental and societal phenomena, or to critique literature. *Literature,* broadly speaking, is anything written for the public to read—from newspaper articles to comic books, encyclopedias to novels. Most English departments, however, divide literature into two broad areas: *nonfiction writing* and *creative writing.*

Nonfiction writing includes essays and books that deal with any topic about which people want to know more. Nonfiction is literature about real people, places, and things, or important ideas, and speaks to the reader directly. Nonfiction forms, also called expository writing, include books on history, philosophy, art, or religion and essays on politics, biology, or astronomy. Authors use nonfiction writing for four major purposes: *to describe, explain, inform,* or *persuade* readers to understand, believe, or agree about something.

Creative writing traditionally covers work done by writers to enlighten or move readers to either laughter or tears, or to the contemplation of a social (e.g., civil rights), philosophical (e.g., What does it mean to be good?), or aesthetic (e.g., What does it mean to be beautiful?) idea. Most college English courses call for reading, criticizing, and analyzing the relative beauty or effectiveness of creative works of literature. Students generally study creative literature in *genres,* or literary forms. These forms include *drama, fiction,* and *poetry.* The following chart, while not exhaustive, should put different forms of literature into perspective for you.

LITERATURE

Nonfiction	Revelation	Creative
Essays or books on:	The Bible	Drama
Business	The Torah	Tragedies
Science	The Koran and	Comedies
Politics	other religious writings attributed	Melodramas
Philosophy	to God	
Religion		Prose
History		Novels and short stories
Letters		
Diaries		Science fiction
Autobiographical prose		Mysteries
		Romances
Research studies		
Essays or books commenting on the arts		Poetry
		Epics and sagas
Docudramas		Lyrical/ballads
Newspaper articles		Songs
		Docudramas

1.3   Why Writing and Reading are Essential Skills

More and more professional, trade, and other careers call for strong writing and reading skills. Many students entering college who are not English majors believe that writing, or knowing how to write, is important only to English majors. However, this is not the case. People in most professions have to present themselves to customers or clients in writing. For instance, scientists must continually read as well as write articles about their research and must write up the results of their experiments. In addition, executives or other professionals must often write memos, reports, proposals, and letters.

It is apparent that secretaries, doctors, lawyers, and civil servants must write. But middle managers, supervisors, vice presidents, and presidents all have to produce excellent writing for their companies and clients—often under short notice. Students may not leave college to write essays about the poetry of Robert Frost or the novels of Ernest Hemingway, but chances are excellent that they will often write for business. Possessing basic and complex writing and reading skills is essential to any competent business or technical professional.

Often, when candidates for a particular job have the same fundamental education, G.P.A., and honors, the job goes to the candidate with the best communication skills. Writing is an essential communication skill. Take a moment and look at the help wanted ads in any newspaper's employment section. Notice how many jobs require the "successful candidate" to have strong writing and other communication skills. In this context, writing can also be seen as a form of power—a form of knowledge without which one would be left behind. The candidate who can write well is promotable, and likely, in the employer's eyes, to be one who can learn and master challenging job tasks.

1.3.1   Writing and Reading as Forms of Learning

Professors know that students who write often and well learn more quickly and remember more than those who write infrequently and poorly. A number of modern scholars have done important research to show that using writing enables an individual to learn about the nature of the world and to gain self-knowledge, as well as to take in and master knowledge in disciplines across the curriculum of college and university courses. Whether the field of study is biology, mapmaking, or computer programming, writing improves learning. To say so of reading goes without question.

Taking notes, recording impressions in a journal, using personal words to describe your experiences—all of these will help any writer to remember and deal with complex experiences and new information better.

1.3.2 Writing and Language Skills Improve Your Reasoning Skills

Students often complain about having to analyze a poem or novel, understand an essay in detail, or take the time to comprehend the false arguments of a demagogue or other political leader. However, reasoning and analytical skills are keys to controlling the way life is led. For instance, failure to comprehend the point of a rule or regulation on the job may lead to dismissal from that job.

The abilities to reason and analyze situations well are not just relevant to mysteries or the complicated plots of novels, but how to solve many of life's problems and how to overcome obstacles. For example, how does one write back to an insurance company that will not pay for earthquake damage in order to be justly compensated? Learn to write (and communicate) well. These are critical life skills that make for an intelligent, informed and rational human being.

1.4 Preparing for a Writing Course

This book is not an exhaustive guide to college writing, grammar, or other related topics. For deep study of particular issues, use course handbooks. Instead, this book is designed to provide a quick review of the meanings and functions of key terms in the study of literature and composition. For example, the precise meaning of "revising" in the writing process can be found in the section of the book called "A Review of the Writing Process."

The student should not read this book as a novel. Instead, he or she should refer to it when a troublesome term or concept arises while preparing an essay or studying. Throughout the text and under the subheadings students will find terms *italicized*. These highlighted terms are the key ideas and definitions needed in college English classes.

Finally, use this book as a supplement to, not a replacement for, course textbooks. Learning from more than one source enhances what the individual remembers and controls. *Don't memorize* the terms; learn them in perspective. Learn them in such a way as to take the concept and *be able to say or restate it differently (paraphrase) while retaining its essential meaning.*

Sheer memorization is the lowest form of learning and only somewhat useful. Those who go into an exam having crammed concepts into memory the night before often panic in the exam room, and they forget much of what they have memorized. However, the student who has learned to use the concepts, to paraphrase, and to apply the terms to his or her reading usually comes out ahead.

Another strategy for learning effectively is to identify the term or concept and then *link the term or concept to an example from personal experience or knowledge that reflects exactly what the concept means.* For example, in fiction, writers often use "stock" characters—that is, character types that seem to show up in life over and over again: the villain, the ingenue (a French term for a young, naive, free-spirited, and virginal woman), or the mad scientist. Other stock characters include: the town drunk, the consoling bartender, the spinster schoolmarm, and so on.

CHAPTER 2

A Brief Review of Reading Skills and the Reading Process

2.1 The Steps of the Active Reading Process

Any course of study in English will inevitably call upon a student to demonstrate and use reading skills successfully. Reading is essential in order to compete effectively in college or in a chosen career. Students must learn or be able to read quickly—often hundreds of pages per day—and retain and comprehend most of what they have read. Reading well is important to all learning activities.

Reading, like writing, is a process that requires active participation during study. Reading at the college level means reading with a view toward at least three results: (1) retaining relevant information, (2) increasing understanding of a discipline or subject, and (3) thinking critically about the truth or accuracy of what has been read.

Although opinions vary on the particular terms, the active reading process may be broken down into five stages: (1) prereading, sometimes called previewing; (2) initial holistic reading; (3) reviewing 1: rereading for thesis, logical development, and content or supporting evidence; (4) reviewing 2: checking for unusual or new vocabulary; and (5) formulating a critical response (agree/disagree; like/ dislike; pro/con, etc.).

2.2 The Initial Reading

During the initial reading, the reader looks for cues. Take the opportunity to get a perspective on what you are about to read. This involves several steps: *deciding on the purpose of the assignment, deciding on the nature of the audience, and scanning, or looking for basic cues about organization from the format, or layout of the piece.*

2.2.1 Determining the Purpose

The reader should first decide on the purpose for reading. In most cases, the purpose of reading will be to learn. While reading may be for fun, to gather support for a personal argument, or even just to pass the time, *always read with a purpose in mind.* Next, determine *the writer's purpose.* Look at the headline or title of the piece to be read. Ask if the writer is trying to *entertain, explain, describe, inform* or *report,* or *persuade* by using argumentation to prove his or her main point or thesis.

Newspapers will use reporting techniques to tell of a plane crash, the events of a distant war, or a local crime. Editors often write *editorials,* or short articles of opinion, in which *the editors express their points of view about a problem or public issue* (e.g., voting for 18-year-olds) and attempt *to persuade the reader that their opinions are the correct ones by arguing with facts, statistics, and other evidence.*

2.2.2 Determining the Probable Audience

Next, in cases in which the audience is most likely not a college student, decide who the intended reader, or audience, is for the piece. Asking a series of questions about a given passage can determine the nature of the audience. While reading, keep in mind the writer's purpose. Using the answers generated by the questions below, *develop a mental "picture" of the audience reading this passage.*

1. What does the writer intend the readers of this passage to take away with them?

2. What is the writer's point of view?

3. How old are the readers?

4. What is their level of education?

5. What is their social or economic class?

6. What attitudes, prejudices, opinions, fears, experiences, and concerns might the audience for this passage have?

Considerations of audience will directly affect the *tone* of a passage, and thus determine what *level of usage or meaning* is appropriate in a given paragraph or section of an essay. *Tone* in expository writing is that *combination of abstract or concrete language; denotation and connotation; jargon, figurative, literal, or plain speech; and simple or complex language that the writer uses to generate a felt response in the reader of some complex attitude the writer has toward a given subject.* To use a simple example, when writing to a 13-year-old, which is more appropriate: "Please peruse with comprehension the tone offered," or "Please be sure to read and understand what is in this book"? The latter sentence, with its simple vocabulary, is the appropriate choice.

2.2.3 Scanning for Basic Features

If the literature is a textbook, read the *introduction,* scan the *chapter titles,* and quickly review any *subheadings, charts, pictures, appendices,* and *indexes* that the book includes. If it is an article, read *the first and last paragraphs* of the article. These are the most likely places to find the writer's *main point* or *thesis.*

Note that there is a significant difference between a thesis and a main point. Here is an example of a *main point:*

> The Rocky Mountains have three important geological features: abundant water, gold- and silver-bearing ore, and oil-bearing shale.

Notice that this statement is not a matter of the writer's opinion. It is a fact. Now, notice the following *thesis:*

> The Rocky Mountains are the most important source of geological wealth in the U.S.A.

What is the difference? The second statement offers an arguable conclusion or informed opinion. It may be an informed opinion on the part of the writer, but it is still an opinion. A *thesis,* then, *is a statement offered by a writer as true, but is actually a matter of opinion.*

In the first statement, whether the author has an opinion about it or not, these features are part of the makeup of the Rocky Mountains. In the second statement, the author may have contrary evidence to offer about Alaska or the Everglades. The second statement requires evidence; the first is self-evident, and the writer would go on to show the existence of these features, not—as in the second case—the quality or value of those features. The writer of a main point paper is reporting or informing his or her audience; the writer of a thesis paper is attempting to sway the audience to his or her point of view.

2.3   Response to Reading

This stage is probably the most enjoyable for the reader. The student should read the article in its entirety. During this reading, *underline* or *highlight* sentences in which the writer makes an important point about his or her thesis.

2.3.1   Distinguishing Between Idea and Evidence

While reading, make a distinction between key ideas and the evidence for those ideas. *Evidence* is anything used to prove that an idea is true. However, only a few forms of evidence are available to the writer. The kinds of evidence that a writer can summon to support his or her position are as follows: (1) facts and statistics, (2) the testimony of authority, (3) personal anecdote, (4) hypothetical illustrations, and (5) analogy. Strictly speaking, the last two in this list are not true evidence, but only offer common sense probability to the support of an argument. In fact, there is a hierarchy for evidence similar to that of purpose. The best evidence is fact, supported by statistics; the least powerful is analogy. The following table suggests the relationship:

HIERARCHY OF VALIDITY OF EVIDENCE

Most Valid	Documented Facts and Statistics
	Expert Testimony
	Personal Experiences and Anecdotes
	Hypothetical Illustrations
Least Valid	Analogies of Any Kind

Documented facts and statistics are the most powerful evidence a writer can bring to bear on proving an idea or supporting a main thesis. Documented facts and statistics must be used fairly and come from reliable sources. Reliable sources include encyclopedias, academic journals, and government publications.

Expert testimony is the reported positions, theses, or studies of people who are recognized experts in the field under discussion. Books, articles, essays, interviews, and so on by trained scientists and other professionals may be used to support a thesis or position. Most often, this testimony takes the form of quotations from the expert or a paraphrasing of his or her important ideas or findings.

Personal anecdote is a writer's own personal experience of an event, person, or idea that exemplifies the point he or she is trying to make.

The experience will serve as evidence if the reader *trusts* the writer, and it is valuable; but it is not as powerful or as conclusive as documented facts or the testimony of experts (unless the writer is a recognized authority in the field about which he or she has written).

Hypothetical illustrations are examples that suggest probable circumstances in which something would be true. Strictly speaking a hypothetical illustration is not "hard" evidence, but, rather evidence of probability. In describing hypothetical situations, the writer is not naming anybody in particular or citing statistics to make the point, but rather is pointing to *a situation that is likely but that is not a documented case.* This situation may have the weight of common sense for the reader, or may carry no weight at all.

Analogy is the last and weakest form of evidence. It is not actually evidence at all. A writer can use an analogy to depict or illustrate deeper meanings and issues by showing a powerful comparison between or among ideas that carries the weight of correctness or aptness for the reader. Analogies are characterized by comparisons and the use of the term "like" to show the relationship of the ideas. (Metaphor and simile, special forms of analogy in literature, are discussed later in this text.) For example, the writer might say, "Life is like a tree: we start out struggling in the dirt, grow into the full bloom of youth, and become deeply rooted in our ways, until, in the autumn of our years, we lose our hair like leaves, and succumb ultimately to the bare winter of death."

While reading, determine what sort of evidence the writer is using and how effective it is in proving his or her point.

2.3.2   Underlining Unusual Words and Phrases

During this stage, unfamiliar words or phrases may appear. Underline them, circle them, or note them in some useful way, and then look them up in a dictionary.

2.4 Reviewing 1: Re-Reading for Thesis, Logical Development, and Content or Supporting Evidence

During this portion of the reading process, review the underlined and highlighted passages for main ideas and for vocabulary. Next determine (1) what the author's main point, or *thesis,* is and where it is stated; (2) what logical patterns the writer uses to organize the article or document (see the list discussed in Chapter 7); and (3) what evidence the writer uses to support his or her position. Commit these findings to memory. Always review as needed; *sometimes several reviews of a difficult chapter or article may be needed, but it is worth doing to gain full comprehension of a text.* There are no shortcuts. The reader must follow this reading process in order to fully understand the text.

2.5 Reviewing 2: Checking for Unusual or New Vocabulary

In this next stage, it is the active reader's job to concentrate on the way the writer is using language. Come to grips with *precise meanings, new terms, and nuances of tone-such as connotation, figurative use of language, and logic.* There is no substitute for accuracy. Often, retention at this stage is indicative of a student's understanding of the entire work.

2.5.1 Using the Dictionary Effectively

Always learn the vocabulary that is new. To learn a word effectively, an individual must engage in several operations.

1. Look up the word in a dictionary of standard English. Good dictionaries also list the *etymology,* or historical source or sources, for the word being researched. Usually, the dictionary will list an abbreviation for the language (e.g., "Fr." for French) from which the word originated. While not always relevant to the way the author has used the word, etymology will always contribute to the total understanding of the word in question.

2. Learn how to pronounce the word correctly. Learn which syllable is most stressed, and how the vowels and consonants are sounded together. In most cases, the dictionary has a *pronunciation guide* either at the beginning or the end of the main word entries. Learn where it is and how to use it.

3. Learn what part of speech the word is (e.g., noun or verb). See Chapter 6 for a fuller discussion and explanation of *parts of speech* in English.

4. Read the meanings and look back at the reading assignment to discover from the context which meaning is the most relevant to the textbook or article; then construct a sentence using the word correctly.

These tasks nearly guarantee permanent knowledge of the word.

2.5.2 Connotation and Denotation

Words not only carry a literal meaning (*denotation*), but also what they bring to mind in the form of *emotional or cultural associations (connotation)*. When reading assignments, try to understand not only what the word literally means, but also how the author might be using it to evoke *a particular set of emotional, social, cultural, or historical associations.* For example, take the word "cheap." The dictionary definition, its denotation or literal meaning, is "not expensive." But the word "cheap" is often associated, or given the implication of being "of poor quality."

Not all connotations are negative. For example, for most people, "house" is literally a dwelling in which a related group of people live. But when the word is changed to "home," even though its actual definition is the same as house, it brings added connotations of warmth, safety, tenderness, and kinship. This is an entire group of positive feelings and associations that are not themselves the "house" in which people live. *When reading, take into account not just what the word means literally, but whether or not the writer is trying to evoke a certain feeling,* as in using "tardy" instead of "late," or "home" instead of "house."

2.5.3   Abstract and Concrete Language

Apart from carrying literal and associative meanings, words can be of two basic types. They indicate that something is either *concrete,* or can be observed directly in a world of space and time or through the senses, or *abstract,* something that is understood only indirectly by association or indirect evidence.

Concrete words embody both qualities. For example, because a pencil can be seen, used, and touched, it can be spoken about concretely. However, there is also the idea of the pencil as a writing tool with graphite, that is sharp at one end, and has an eraser at the other. In the second case, a particular pencil may not be indicated. It has been used to point out a type, class, or species of that thing: pencils in general, pencils in the abstract. Concrete words carry both concrete and abstract possibilities, while abstractions can only be understood indirectly.

Feelings, ideas, and notions cannot be directly observed, but can be understood only indirectly. For example, a kiss may be evidence of love, but we can observe only the kiss directly, not the love. The love is assumed. Other examples of abstractions are hate, truth, beauty, and friendship.

2.6   Formulating A Critical Response

Once the text has been preread, read, reviewed, and checked for vocabulary, a critical response may be formulated. Comprehension of a text calls for evaluation of what has been read. To *assess* a piece of literature, read the piece with an understanding of what its purpose is and how it develops logically to make its point. To *evaluate* a piece of literature, make a case for a personal but informed judgment about its relative success or failure in terms of its logic, its adequate development, and its relative use of literary or writing skills.

Of course, everyone is entitled to his or her own opinion about any piece of writing or set of ideas. However, in a college setting, students are often held responsible for making a case for what they think about a piece of writing, not just what they feel or opine about it. It can be said that "This essay is convincing;" but merely saying so or *asserting an opinion* doesn't make it real, true, or even probable. In college, as elsewhere in life, use reasoning skills to determine the relative validity, aptness, or truth of what the author has presented.

2.6.1 Implications and Inferences

When writers present ideas, conclusions about what they are saying based on the *implications,* or possible related ideas or positions consistent with their central idea, can be made. Ideas suggest other ideas, and as long as the ideas are logically consistent with the author's central point, the reader may assume that the writer would probably go along with these related ideas.

Writers sometimes *imply* things that would be a logical extension of what they actually say. Read this brief sample passage:

> (E) I want a house that has no plumbing. (E) I want a house that looks out at the mountains. (E) I want a house that has rough cut walls and woodstove heat. (E) I want a house that has open country for a backyard and a lake view for a front yard. (E) I want a house with no neighbors but the birds, the bears, and the wild creatures of the earth.

It would be unreasonable to suggest that the writer in this passage is implying that he wants to live in a well-serviced industrial, urban environment. It doesn't logically fit the examples (E's) he offers in his paragraph. One of the implications of this is clearly that the writer wants to live in just the opposite environment. A real implication based on this passage is that this writer would rather live near animals than near people. Notice that the paragraph lists examples as evidence for the writer's point of view. All of the sentences exemplify characteristics of the "house" this writer wants—but not one of them is conclusive. So, this writer **implies, without actually stating,** the kind of "home" he wants. Yet, the reader still gets a clear picture or idea of where this writer's home would be set.

Although he doesn't say it, the point of the paragraph is this:

[The writer] wants a home in the wilderness. (**T**)

This would be the thesis (**T**) sentence of this writer's paragraph or passage if he had not implied it, but had instead stated it. There is a sense that the writer hates people—but **be careful:** that's what the reader may feel, not what the writer is implying. *Don't confuse feelings with the writer's facts or illustrations.*

Professors will often require students to understand and recognize what they can *infer* from the passage once they have read it. Actually, implications and inferences are very similar; the only difference is who is making them: *Writers imply; readers infer.* For example, with the example used above, the reader could infer that the writer is a person who probably likes the outdoors, camping, and even hunting. That's an *inference:* a reader's *probable* and *reasonable* conclusion or interpretation of an idea based upon what the writer has written.

2.6.2 Logic: Induction, Deduction, and Fallacies

In formulating critical evaluations of a piece of writing, professors may wish students to understand the problems, if any, with the logic of the piece they have read. Does it make sense? If not, why doesn't it? It is up to the reader to find the errors in any piece of writing he or she reads. Of course, if the writer is effective, the reader won't find these fallacies. Be on the lookout for them, because it is often a good way to refute, criticize, or counterargue if called upon to respond critically to any author's central idea, thesis, or main point. Make sure the evidence proves the writer's point and not something else.

Pay special attention to conclusions. The writer may not have proved the point. An essay is essentially a syllogism that proves something by induction or deduction. The syllogism is that basic form of deductive reasoning that is the cornerstone of most logic. It consists of a major premise, a minor premise, and a conclusion. Note how they are used in the following discussion. Induction is the sort of reasoning which arrives at a general conclusion based on the relationship among the contributing elements of an idea.

For example, a writer may observe under experimental conditions that whenever a spider begins to spin a web, it first rubs its back legs over its silk gland. The author may have observed 100,000 different species of spiders display this behavior. He or she may have also observed that they never rub their hind legs over the gland at any other time, only when they are about to put out silk to start a web. He or she may then induce from these observations that spiders must rub their hind legs over their silk glands in order to begin the production of silk to spin a web. Another individual may prove this theory wrong later, because new evidence shows up to invalidate the induction; until that happens, this though, will be the conclusion drawn from observations of the behavior of spiders.

Deduction, by way of contrast, reasons from the general to the particular. For example, an author may assert that all trees grow upward from the earth, not downward from the sky. Until someone finds a tree that grows from the sky to the earth, an individual will assume that every tree started growing out of the earth, and base all other conclusions about the growth and flowering of trees upon this *deduction* as well.

Occasionally, however, the *premises* of a deductive argument are false or unprovable. The *premises* of an argument are those *definitions* or *assumptions* that are givens (concepts which do not stand in need of proof but are either self-evident, common knowledge, or agreed upon as terms between the writer and the reader). For example,

Major Premise: All goats have beards.

Minor Premise: Harry Jones has a beard.

Conclusion: Therefore, Harry is a goat.

The conclusion is correct and logical *based on the premises,* or definitions or assumptions offered in this case, but the premises are selective. What about the fact that Harry is a human being and that goats are not human beings? These are mutually exclusive. Thus, Harry cannot be a goat.

2.6.3 Typical Logical Fallacies

Below is a list of typical logical errors that weak writers commit. The list is not exhaustive. Know how they occur and practice finding them in others' arguments, either in conversation or in essays they may have written.

1. *Either/or:* The writer assumes only two opposing possibilities: "Either we abolish cars, or the environment is doomed." Other factors may contribute to the destruction of the environment.

2. *Oversimplification:* Here, the author might first state, "Only motivated athletes become champions." Perhaps not; though unfortunate, athletes who use enhancing steroids occasionally become champions, too.

3. *Begging the question:* The writer assumes he or she has proved something which has not been proven. "He is unintelligent because he is stupid." A lack of intelligence is almost synonymous with being stupid; it cannot be proven that he is stupid by saying he is unintelligent; that "he" is either or both of these is exactly what needs to be proved.

4. *Ignoring the issue:* An argument against the truth of a person's testimony in court shifts from what the witness observed to how the witness's testimony is inadmissible because the witness is obviously unkempt and homeless. One has nothing to do with the other.

5. *Arguing against a person, not an idea:* The writer argues that somebody's idea has no merit because he or she is immoral or unintelligent: "John can't prove anything about dogs being faithful; he can't even understand basic mathematics."

6. *"It does not follow…" or Non Sequitur:* The writer leaps to a wrong conclusion: "John is tall; he must know a lot about mountains."

7. *Drawing the wrong conclusion from a sequence:* "He trained and then read and then trained some more and therefore won the match." It is quite possible that other factors led to his winning the match.

2.7 The Power and Types of Reading in College

Reading well and with control is essential to a successful college career. Not all students will need coursework in reading per se. However, during a college career, the student's ability to understand reading material will make an enormous difference in how well he or she performs, not to mention the degree to which the student can learn a fact or even a given discipline.

Reading creative literature, while essentially the same *process* as non-creative literature, takes on particular characteristics and a particular jargon—or special vocabulary—which students are required to work with and understand. Every time a new discipline is learned or a new field of study is entered, new vocabulary needs to be mastered. The study of creative literature in college English courses involves the mastery of a special vocabulary by the student. The chapters ahead will examine much more deeply the special vocabulary used for the study of creative literature and how to understand and apply it in college courses that deal with literature as a creative art, rather than those college courses that deal with literature principally as expository prose that conveys information or opinion. First, however, the student must understand and control the other major process in college English: the writing process.

Problem Solving Example:

Q Read the following essay and answer the questions that follow.

A **Education of Women**
We do not think a classical education proper for women. It may pervert their minds, but it cannot elevate them. It has been asked, Why a woman should not learn the dead languages as well as the modern ones?

5 For this plain reason, that the ones are still spoken, and may have immediate associations connected with them, and the other not. A woman may
have a lover who is a Frenchman, or an Italian, or a Spaniard; and it is
well to be provided against every contingency in that way. But what
possible interest can she feel in those old-fashioned persons, the Greeks
10 and Romans, or in what was done two thousand years ago? A modern
widow would doubtless prefer Signor Tramezzani to Aeneas, and Mr.
Conway would be a formidable rival to Paris.[1] No young lady in our days,
in conceiving an idea of Apollo, can go a step beyond the image of her
favorite poet: nor do we wonder that our old friend, the Prince Regent,[2]
15 passes for a perfect Adonis in the circles of beauty and fashion. Women in
general have no ideas, except personal ones. They are mere egoists. They
have no passion for truth, nor any love of what is purely ideal. They hate to
think, and they hate every one who seems to think of anything but themselves. Everything is to them a perfect nonentity which does not
20 touch their senses, their vanity, or their interest. Their poetry, their criti-
cism, their politics, their morality, and their divinity, are downright affec-
tation. That line in Milton is very striking—

'He for God only, she for God in him.'

Such is the order of nature and providence; and we should be sorry to
25 see any fantastic improvements on it. Women are what they were meant to
be; and we wish for no alteration in their bodies or their minds. They are
the creatures of the circumstances in which they are placed, of sense, of
sympathy and habit. They are exquisitely susceptible of the passive impressions of things: but to form an idea of pure understanding or imagination,
30 to feel an interest in the true and the good beyond themselves, requires an
effort of which they are incapable. They want principle, except that which
consists in an adherence to established custom; and this is the reason of the
severe laws which have been set up as a barrier against every infringement of
decorum and propriety in women. It has been observed by an ingenious
35 writer of the present day, that women want imagination. This requires
explanation. They have less of that imagination which depends on intensity
of passion, on the accumulation of ideas and feelings round one object, on

---

[1] Hazlitt was a theatre critic and had accused a popular Italian tenor, Tramezzani, of overacting in his love
scenes. He also criticized actor William Conway in the role of Romeo.
[2] The Prince Regent was George, Prince of Wales, recently declared insane.

bringing all nature and all art to bear on a particular purpose, on continuity and comprehension of mind; but for the same reason, they have more fancy, that is greater flexibility of mind, and can more readily vary and separate
40 their ideas at pleasure. The reason of the greater presence of mind which has been remarked in women is, that they are less in the habit of speculating on what is best to be done, and the first suggestion is decisive. The writer of this article confesses that he never met with any woman who could reason, and with but one reasonable woman. There is no instance of a woman
45 having been a great mathematician or metaphysician or poet or painter: but they can dance and sing and act and write novels and fall in love, which last quality alone makes more than angels of them. Women are no judges of the characters of men, except as men. They have no real respect for men, or they never respect them for those qualities, for which they are respected by
50 men. They in fact regard all such qualities as interfering with their own pretensions, and creating a jurisdiction different from their own. Women naturally wish to have their favourites all to themselves, and flatter their weaknesses to make them more dependent on their own good opinion, which, they think, is all they want. We have, indeed, seen instances of men,
55 equally respectable and amiable, equally admired by the women and es-teemed by the men, but who have been ruined by an excess of virtues and accomplishments.

—William Hazlitt (1815)

Here is an opportunity to use the skills you've read about in the chap-ter; imagine that your purpose for reading is assigned work in a His-tory or English course. Follow the sequence of skills discussed.

 Read the first and last paragraphs and suggest a possible audi-ence, and your reason for why it would be such an audience.

 A quick look over the text of "Education of Women" reveals a few items worth mentioning. This short essay is probably most closely related to an Op-Ed (Opinion-Editorial) piece written in a news-paper. Published in the *Examiner* in 1815, the essay begins with a proc-lamation, "We do not think a classical education proper for women." The term "we" suggests the assurance of numbers and power. It's safe to assume Hazlitt speaks for a significant group (perhaps educated men?).

And lastly, the year 1815 is relevant to our reading because it suggests a time when women did not enjoy the rights and privileges that are commonplace today, at least in most major industrialized cultures.

 Scan the essay, noting the length and number of paragraphs, and the general handling of the content. Mark the important sentences and phrases, including the thesis and supporting information.

 The essay seems to be argumentative, that is, it seeks to convince. The essay's very first sentence is its thesis, a statement offered as fact but is really opinion. Each of the paragraphs contains sentences of this type, assertions that explain the author's position on the subject. Other examples include the sentences beginning on line 14: "Women in general," or line 16: "They hate to think," or line 47: "Women are no judges." There are also many cases of phrases within sentences that offer good examples of the author's viewpoint.

 Evaluate the validity of the evidence provided by distinguishing between ideas and evidence; is the information based on research or citations from reference sources, or is personal experience the central source of the author's findings?

 An analysis examines a whole as the sum of its parts. Another brief look at the outline of "Education of Women" reveals the parts of Hazlitt's argument. In short, women should not be educated because they lack the qualities education enhances. They lack the capacity to entertain ideas because they have no passion for truth and hate to think. Women are naturally predisposed to acting precipitously rather than thoughtfully, without the use of reasoning. Evidence for these statements may be found in the lack of female contributions to human knowledge. Women can "perform" (and write novels, a less-than-respectable literary endeavor in 1815), and fall in love, but do little else. In short, things that require judgment are not suitable activities for women.

Hazlitt's essay has a rather simple argumentative structure. He asserts women are not educable and then provides "reasons" why. Hazlitt's "reasons" are primarily opinions, offered without evidence except the assertion that women have achieved little. The essay concludes with final comment on the ability of women to ruin men, chiefly through flattery.

Analysis reveals that Hazlitt's essay has little to offer in support of the opinion it presents. Further, its statements seem more an emotional outpouring than a reasonable explanation. (The careful reader will also make note of how difficult it is to view Hazlitt's remarks in an unprejudiced fashion—the contemporary reader will, in all probability, find his assertions a bit ridiculous.)

 Are there any unfamiliar words? Where do you find concrete and abstract language, and what are their effects in the essay?

 Hazlitt includes allusions to literary and historical figures, and displays his education by including a quotation from Milton.

Regarding concrete and abstract language, Hazlitt tends toward the abstract, since his essay is concerned with issues, such as equality, morals, intellectual ability, and education, rather than with objects.

 Lastly, what is your critical response to the essay? How does it use inference and implication? Does the author construct a logical argument? Why or why not?

 Naturally, every reader's response to any piece of writing will be unique. At the same time, however, while nineteenth-century readers would probably have nodded in agreement as Hazlitt offered reasons why women shouldn't be educated, contemporary readers might more readily become surprised, dismayed, or perhaps even angry. Review your responses in the annotations to the text. They will help recreate your personal reactions and the causes for those reactions. Do not always expect to agree with, or even appreciate, a writer's point of view. You will find yourself disagreeing with texts rather frequently. The important thing is to be certain you can account for the sources and causes of your disagreement. Much of our disagreement with Hazlitt's essay rests in what we would consider a more enlightened perspective on the abilities of women. An awareness of historical context does help explain "Education of Women," but probably doesn't increase our sympathy for Hazlitt's position.

CHAPTER 3

Working with the Writing Process

3.1 Review of the Writing Process

In their exploration into how people write in English, recent researchers have placed considerable emphasis on understanding the writing process. Those who know how to process their writing generally are, or become, better writers. What is the best way to proceed? Although scholars vary on some of the details, and even some of the terms, most instructors of composition and writing courses in college have students spend time understanding how the writing process works and employing the process to write papers.

Basically, the writing process does not consist of the writing of the introduction, body, and conclusion. Those sections of the *product* must appear in the format of the final version of any expository paper, but those formal sections do not reflect the stages of the *process* any writer must go through in order to produce the resulting final copy of the essay. Furthermore, writers recommend that students go through these stages in the sequence they are presented here in order to begin easily, write effectively, check for problems, and complete the paper. Following these steps in order is as important to good writing as the topic of the paper. The writing process includes six basic stages:

OUTLINE OF THE WRITING PROCESS

Prewriting: Choosing a topic; getting ideas on paper quickly: brainstorming, freewriting, clustering; interviewing; researching; deciding on the purpose and audience, and employing other techniques for summoning ideas relevant to the paper's topic.

Outlining: Organizing ideas into a logical sequence or pattern.

Drafting: Writing the paper from the prewriting notes without regard to precise logic, editing, or proofreading. A fast bringing-forth of ideas.

Revising: Checking the paper for logic, organization, purpose, relevant content, correct format, paragraphs, and "flow" and making adjustments and changes as necessary.

Editing: Controlling sentence structure, style, punctuation, spelling, and making changes as necessary.

Proofreading: Correcting the paper for common typos, format, and spelling errors.

3.2   Time Management

Time management of the writing process is the way the writer utilizes time during the writing process in order to meet the course deadline for a given paper. Effective prewriting, drafting, revising, editing, and proofreading are important to get the paper done on time. College deadlines are no different from other deadlines in life. A college graduate's career will continue to require that work is done on time. Learning to use the writing process effectively and expediently will prove to be a great asset.

3.3 Prewriting

Prewriting begins when a student chooses a topic and collects thoughts in preparation for writing a given composition or research paper. Prewriting offers many possible techniques for choosing a topic and getting started with writing.

3.3.1 Choosing a Topic

Many professors will assign topics to write about; others will allow students to choose their own topics. A *topic* is any subject of study, inquiry, or discussion that is addressed for the sake of an audience. A topic, however, is not a main point or a thesis. Remember that a *topic* is the subject about which the author writes. Books, cars, people, sports, *anything* can be a topic of inquiry, study, or discussion. The point is to choose one and begin to focus on writing about it.

In college, the topics you choose or are assigned to write about will be quite complicated and will require subtle and involved essay-writing skills. It is rare that you will encounter a topic that can be satisfactorily answered in less than five typed pages. However, for this book, in the interest of clearly defining the writing process, we have chosen a simple topic that can be answered in a shorter essay.

Some topics are too broad to deal with in a short 500 word essay, so the professor may ask that the topic be narrowed. *Narrowing a topic means limiting it and becoming more specific about what is to be discussed in the paper, making it a manageable length and scope.* For example, suppose the chosen topic is "books." Before writing, decide on the *purpose* in writing and the *audience* that is going to read the work. Although the professor is the immediate audience, he or she may allow a choice in audience. If this is the case, decide on some relevant characteristics that the readers may have.

Problem Solving Example:

 Your English composition professor has assigned you the topic "college" for your next essay. He has asked you to narrow your topic to one aspect of college.

You narrow the topic to one specific aspect of college—adapting to college life.

3.3.2 Getting Ideas on Paper Quickly

For students, often the most difficult question in writing is how to begin. There are several techniques for getting started. This section explores three or four of the major ones available. In the reading process, the reader must determine what his or her purpose for reading is and what the writer's purpose for writing is.

Similarly, in the writing process, the writer must decide what the purpose for writing is going to be. This technique will help the writer get started and, at the same time, will help narrow down the topic. What does the author want to explain when writing about "books"? Does the author wish to describe—that is, talk about what physical qualities the books possess; explain what they are, inform readers about some issue or quality about them, or to persuade readers about something in relation to "books"?

More often than not, the professor will ask students to *persuade* the reader(s) of something about the topic. This calls for the use of *argumentation,* or persuasive composition, to make the point. (See Chapter 4 for a detailed discussion of argumentation.)

Suppose the writer wants to persuade the reader that reading books is a waste of time. *Audience* is the next important consideration. The writer must decide on the person or group of people that would, or should, be persuaded by the argument. Once the author determines the audience, his or her focus for persuasion changes. *Audience awareness often determines the direction and content of writing.* If a student attempts to persuade his/her professor that reading books is a waste of time, then he or she will have to summon a great deal of information since most professors would disagree.

It would be impossible, however, to discuss in a 500-word essay, or even in a short research paper, how reading any book is a waste of time. The subject of discussion needs to be narrowed even further. The way to do this is to use specific adjectives to condense the field of thinking and discussion. Thus, instead of claiming that reading is a waste of time, leaving open an encyclopedia of trouble, narrow the field to:

> Reading history textbooks is a waste of time for college students.

Admittedly, however, *some* college students will not find reading history textbooks to be a waste of time. Therefore, do not claim that this statement is true for all by not *qualifying the thesis.* Instead, narrow the topic even further:

> Many history textbooks are a waste of time for college students.

Obviously, this topic can be narrowed even further.

Through a technique called *freewriting,* the writer can also begin the writing process. Freewriting is putting down on paper whatever comes to mind at the time. When utilizing this technique, be sure not to worry about technical matters such as spelling, punctuation, paragraphing, etc. The writer often develops interesting and novel ideas during this stage. The important aspect about freewriting is the "flow" of the writing, however imperfect the technical aspects of sentence structure and grammar may be at the moment. Correcting these errors comes later in the process.

Problem Solving Example:

 Your English composition professor has asked you to begin by freewriting on your topic. What might your freewriting look like?

Your freewriting might look like this.

Adapting to College Life

My first day of college mixed emotions. Leaving home at 4:00 a.m. to be at the college at 10:00 a.m. The car was full of boxes, suitcases and clothes on hangers. We spent six hours on the road, At the college, cars, station wagons, and RVs were everywhere—all full of boxes, suitcases, and clothes on hangers just like mine. Parents were helping their sons and daughters move in. Upperclassmen too were helping. There were grocery carts for us to put our belongings in to take then to our rooms. My rommate Marcia arrived first. Her boxes were already in the room. She decided to take the right half of the room. That left me the left side. We uppacked while our parents chatted. Then,. my mother put ther sheets and bedspread on my bed. I guess this was her last motherly dduty before I became indenpendent. After unpapcking, I met with my advisor dr. Ridge from the Department of English. He saw I was scared, so he asked me sit in the Boston rocker in his office. Slowly, he went over the list of courses being offered and helped me pick out the I would need. He keyed my registrstion into the computer and gave me a copy. Then, I was off to the bookstore. Students everywhere. I got lost trying to find all the textbooks that I needed and ended up in the anatomy section. Once at the check out line, The cashier said that would be $266.50. She looked at me, smiled, said freshman and just laughed, saying by the time you get to be a senior your books will double in cost. I quickly paid her, and ran all the way back to my dorm rrom with a heavy load of books in my arms. I knew I has had the worst mistake of my life.

3.3.3 Brainstorming

Brainstorming is the technique by which the author takes a few minutes to list, in random order, all the ideas and thoughts he or she has about a topic. When brainstorming a topic, the writer acts as a reporter would act and uses the *reporter's heuristic* for getting the "lead" to the story. A good reporter asks key questions of any event in order to write the "lead" or beginning to a story: What happened? Who was there? When did it happen? How did it happen? Where did it happen? Why did it happen? When confronting a topic, the writer asks similar related questions of the topic and writes down the answers to the relevant questions as quickly as he or she can think of them. The author must simply write down ideas as they come out and not censor them. By the end of this process the writer will have conceived many ideas and concepts.

Problem Solving Example:

 Next, your professor asks you to brainstorm for a list of possible ideas and questions about your topic. What might your list look like?

Below is the list of ideas and questions you generated:

Adapting to College Life

a.   Leaving home at 4:00 a.m. to be at the college by 10: 00 a.m.

b.   Mothers and fathers bringing sons and daughters to college.

c.   RVs, trailers, and station wagons loaded down with boxes and suitcases.

d.   Grocery carts in the parking lot for freshman to use to transport their belongings from their vehicle to their dorm room.

e.   Why did I ever decide to go a college far away from home?

f.   Upperclassman helping freshmen.

g.   Dorm elevators very slow.

h.   Roommate from out of state

i.   Will we get along?

j.   How to I learn to share a living space after having my own room for eighteen years?

k. My mother putting the sheets and the bedspread on my dorm room bed.

l. Dividing the room, furniture, and closet space.

m. Where will I plug my computer in?

n. Registering for classes.

o. Taking placement tests in English grammar and math.

p. How do I decide what classes to take?

q. Meeting with my advisor.

r. Schedule hard to understand.

s. Book store crowded.

t. Books are expensive.

u. Cashier laughs at me.

v. Books weigh a lot and hard to carry back to dorm.

w. Finding my way around campus.

x. Know I am going to get lost and end up in some place where no one can find me.

y. Fear.

z. Did I make a right decision?

3.3.4 Clustering

Clustering involves writing a topic in the center of a piece of paper around which the writer lists all the things about the topic that he or she can think of, thus creating little "rays" of thought that stem from the topic.

Below is an illustration of how this might look.

CLUSTERING: A PREWRITING TECHNIQUE

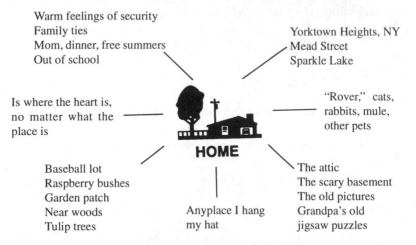

Warm feelings of security
Family ties
Mom, dinner, free summers
Out of school

Yorktown Heights, NY
Mead Street
Sparkle Lake

Is where the heart is,
no matter what the
place is

"Rover," cats,
rabbits, mule,
other pets

HOME

Baseball lot
Raspberry bushes
Garden patch
Near woods
Tulip trees

Anyplace I hang
my hat

The attic
The scary basement
The old pictures
Grandpa's old
jigsaw puzzles

Problem Solving Example:

 The professor asks you to apply the process of clustering to your topic. What might the result look like?

 The illustration below shows how your clustering might look.

Adapting to College Life

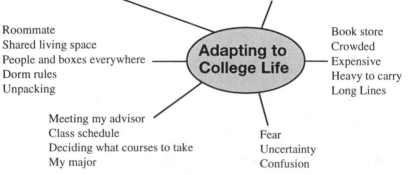

Leaving home
Sad and happy at the same time

Learning to be independent
Mom's advice

Roommate
Shared living space
People and boxes everywhere
Dorm rules
Unpacking

Adapting to College Life

Book store
Crowded
Expensive
Heavy to carry
Long Lines

Meeting my advisor
Class schedule
Deciding what courses to take
My major

Fear
Uncertainty
Confusion

3.4   Interviewing

Interviewing is as it suggests: getting useful information from friends, colleagues, or people "in the know." This prewriting technique often helps to give direction to the writer. Of course, writers should take notes when interviewing. Some students prefer to use a tape recorder during the interview and take notes from the tape later.

3.5   Researching

Researching is the process of using primary and secondary sources of information to find out about a given topic. Some topics demand statistics or documented evidence for proof. Use the library and other public sources of information for this type of proof.

3.6   Outlining

Preparing an outline is the next logical step in writing a paper. It requires only a short time to prepare, and helps tremendously when actually writing the paper. Writing a paper without an outline is like taking a walk through a strange city without a map. The destination might be reached, but only by chance. With a map, the traveler can know the way in advance. Similarly, an outline is a plan; it guides the writer through the paper by clear and logical steps.

When writing an outline, you should note all thoughts on the subject in short phrases, considering whether they contribute to the purpose and point of the paper. For example, you might want to explain what surfing is and why it is enjoyable. The following thoughts might occur:

Surfing is fun
you need a board
what the board is made of
length and weight of the board
how to learn
where surfing came from
you can surf on Long Island, but it is better in Hawaii

The next step is organization. First, group the ideas. Many entries concern the board. Group them under a main heading called "The Board." Then four other points remain: surfing is fun, learning to surf, history of surfing, and good places to surf. Along with "The Board," these become the main points, because they cannot be grouped under any other heading. These are the major headings; all other points will fall under one of them.

These main points must be organized. The order must be logical to both you and the reader. They should develop, or work toward, and end.

The following is a sample outline for the surfing paper:

Introduction

History of surfing

The board

    why you need it

    its length and weight

How to learn to surf

Surfing is fun

Best places to surf

Now, in looking over the outline, you might decide to spend the major part of your paper discussing the board and how to learn and might make the last two sections rather short. Or, you might decide to make all the sections about the same length, except the first one, which should be relatively short because it is a general introduction to the paper. Decisions of this nature should be made before any writing is attempted.

Your outline should be structured in a precise manner. An outline is a chart of subjects, branching from the general to the increasingly specific. The broadest topics are indicated with uppercase Roman numerals and begin at the left margins. The largest subtopics of these are placed beneath them, indented five spaces and sequenced by uppercase letters. Subtopics of subtopics become increasingly narrow, continuing from subjects that are numbered with Arabic numerals, to those followed by lowercase letters, and finally to lowercase Roman numerals, each indented an additional five spaces from the left margin. Roman numerals are given extra indentation to give equally-ranked topics the same starting point at the left. Each numeral and letter marking is followed by a period and two spaces. The following fictitious biography outline demonstrates the outline format:

I. Childhood
    A. Parentage
    B. War Years
       1. Hardships
          a. poverty
          b. family
             i.   brother enlists, dies
             ii. parents die in bombing
             iii. siblings distributed
       2. early accomplishments
II. Adulthood
    A. Writing Career
       1. early struggle
       2. success
          a. first recognition
          b. rise to fame
       3. later works
    B. Family
       1. marriage
       2. offspring
    C. Death

Each topic should have either zero subtopics or at least two subtopics. Never give an "A/a" without a "B/b" or an "I/1/i" without a "II/2/ii." When you find that you have six or more subtopics of equal rank under the same topic, stop to consider whether they should be under two different topics. Note that only the two highest subtopic rankings are capitalized, and that no level of the outline is more than a sentence fragment.

Problem Solving Example:

 You decide to write an outline to help organize your ideas. How might your outline look?

 The following is an example of a possible outline for this paper.

I. Arriving at College
    A. Driving to college
    B. Finding out how different it is from home
        1. Sharing a dorm room
            a. meeting the roommate
            b. dividing the furniture
        2. Sharing a bathroom
            a. bathroom using schedule
            b. bathroom cleaning schedule.
II. Getting ready for classes
    A. Meeting the advisor
        1. He's comforting
            a. like a grandfather
            b. the Boston rocker
        2. Choosing classes
            a. college survival skills
                i. required course
                ii. will help me adapt
            b. Freshman composition
            c. Calculus
            d. Japanese I
    B. The book store
        1. It is huge
            a. aisles and aisles crowded with students
            b. getting lost

              i. in the anatomy section

            ii. an upperclassman helps me

      2. The books are expensive

         a. $260.50 for books for five classes

         b. the books will cost more later in college

III.   Starting to feel better

    A. Talking to mom

        1. Admitting I'm scared

          a. crying

          b. telling her I want to come home

        2. Her advice

          a. she had felt the same way

          b. I'll make my roommate homesick

          c. if I go home now I may never leave home

    B. Deciding to be strong

        1. College was where I needed to be

        2. Talking to roommates

          a. going through connecting bathroom

          b. offering popcorn and soap operas

        3. I'll be fine at Brevard College

3.7 Drafting

Drafting is the stage in the writing process during which the writer uses all the information gathered from prewriting, from the outline, and from his or her audience awareness notes in order to write about the topic at hand. Like freewriting, drafting allows writing without censorship and without worrying about the regulations and details of writing itself.

Drafting is not unlike writing a letter to a long absent friend. That's what rough drafting is: telling readers the "news," providing them with information relevant to the topic. The writer has completed the draft when he or she determines that there is nothing more to say, after having reviewed the prewriting notes and the outline. If something is thought of later, the writer should add it to the draft where it fits best. In this stage of the writing process, the writing is fast and messy. This is no reason for concern. These trouble spots will be taken care of in the next stage: revising.

Problem Solving Example:

Your professor asks you to write a draft. What might the draft look like?

Your draft might look like this, with some notes you might make to yourself regarding possible revisions:

Adapting to College Life

My life changed when I went to college. I had to learn to be indapendent. At home, I had my own room and bath, and I could go to my parents for advice. Now, at college, I had a roomate, shared a bathroom with 3 other people, and no won to depend on but myself.

Learning to share a living space was hard. My roommate and I spent over two hours discussing who should get what bed, dreser, closet, book shelveses and desk. I shared it with my roommate and the two girls in the room. The four of us had to decide on a mourning bathroom schedule based upon who had the earlier class, and we had to device a weekly bathroom cleanning. It took me several weeks to adjust to sharing my living space and my bathroom.

If I had a problem, I could no longer go to my parants. Instead, I had an advisor to handle it. My advisor was an instructor in the Department of english. He was an older gentlemen, who spoke more like a grandfather than a stranger. In his office, he had a Boston rocker. At our first meeting, he told me to sit in the chair, and said Ellen, rocking will make you less nervous he helped to decide what courses to take as well as how to read the college's schedule. He went on to say that the required course for freshmen, College Survival Skills, would help me with my adjust to college life. He logged my registration for College Survival Skills into his computer. Then, we discussed what other courses I should take. We agreed on western civilization, freshman composition

I, calculus, and japanese I, which he logged into his computer. When he was done, he handed me a copy of my schedule and said, "Come by as often as often as you like. Remember, I am here to help you."

Afterwards, I had to go to the bookstore to purchase my books. The bookstore was huge and crowded with students. It looked like a big department store at the mall. Instead of clothes and accessories, it had isles and isles of books for every subject being offered at the college. It took me over two hours to find my books. I got lost in the aisles and ended up in the anatomy section when I searched for the textbook for my Japanese class. An upper classman had to point me to the textbook for my Japanese class. After finding my books, I went to the cashier. After she scanned the bar code on each book, she said, "honey, that will be $260.50."

I responded, "Over $200 for five books for five classes?"

Yes she replied, "and the books will cost you more the further along you get in college.

I roped my check and headed back to the dorm. As soon as I got to my room, I called my mother and sobbed, "Mom, I've made a big mistake. College isn't for me. I want to come home.

In a kind voice, she responded, "Ellen, your staying. College is where you need to be. I called my my Mother, your Grandmother, and said the same thing. She gave me two peaces of advise: First, don't cry. You live closer to home than your roommate If you're home sick, your roommate will get home sick to. And second, you are acting just like a girl who was in college with me. When this girl asked to come home after just moving into her dorm room, her parents packed up all her belongings and moved her back home. The girl is still living with her parents some twenty-five years later. Your now independent; you can't turn back."

I turned the portable telephone off and thought, "if I could learn how to share, plane the classes I should take, and survive the college bookstore, then I could handle anything that lie ahead. College was wear I did need to be."

I laid the telephone down, dashed through the conecting bathroom, to ask my new freinds, "Does anyone want to ate microwave popcorn and watch the afternoon soaps with me?"

I tucked my mother's words away safely in my heart.   I new I would do just find at brevard collage.

3.8   Revising

Revising occurs each time a concept in the rough draft is changed, rearranged, or altered. Be sure to examine the *organization, paragraphing, scope and nature of the thesis,* or *format* (the appearance and layout of the paper). This is the step and time in the process when *transitions, flow,* and the *logic* of the paper are analyzed. Revise before editing, and remember to keep paragraphs short and concise. This may entail moving whole paragraphs from one place to another within the text, adding a transition, or cutting out whole paragraphs. Continue this process until the paper logically supports the thesis.

Problem Solving Example:

 Your professor asks you to revise your paper. He asks you to look at your organization, paragraphing and scope. How might your revision look ?

 Below is how your revised copy might look.

Adapting to College Life

My life changed when I went to Brevard College. I had to learn to be indapendent. At home, I had my own room and bath, and I could go to my parents for advise. Now, at college, I had a roomate, shared a bathroom with 3 other people, and no one to depend on but myself.

Learning to share a living space was hard. At my home in North Carolina, I had my own bedroom. Now, I was sharing a dormitory room with a girl from New Jersey. My roommate and I spent over two hours discussing who should get what bed, dreser, closet, book shelveses and desk.

Next, came the bathroom. At home, I had my own private bath-room, and I could spread out my shampoo and cosmetics all over the vanity. Now, my bathroom connected to the next dormitory room, and I shared it with my roommate and the two girls in the next room. The four of us had to decide on a mourning bathroom schedule based upon who had the earlier class, and we had to devise a weakly bathroom cleanning schedule. It took me several weeks to adjust to sharing my living space and my bathroom.

If I had a problem, I could no longer go to my parants. Instead, I had an advisor to handle it. My advisor was an instructor in the De-partment of english. He is an older gentlemen, who spoke more like a grandfather than a stranger. In his office, he had a Boston rocker. At our first meeting, he told me to sit in the chair, and said, Ellen, rocking will make you less nervous. He helped me to decide what courses to take as well as how to read the college's schedule. He went on to say the required course for freshmen, College Survival Skills, would help me with my adjust to college life. He logged my registration for Col-lege Survival Skills into his computer. Then, we discussed what other courses I should take. We agreed on western civilization, freshman composition I, calculus, and japanese I, which he logged into his com-puter. When he was done, he handed me a copy of my schedule and said, "Come by as often as often as you like. Remember, I am here to help you."

Afterwards, I had to go to the bookstore to purchase my books. The bookstore was huge and crowded with students. It looked like a big department store at the mall. Instead of cloths and accessories, it had isles and isles of books for every subject being offered at the col-lege. It took me over two hours to find my books. I got lost in the aisles and ended up in the medical school section when I searched for the textbook for my Japanese class. A medical student had to point me to the textbook for my Japanese class. After finding my books, I went to the cashier. After she scanned the bar code on each book, she said, "honey, that will be $260.50."

I responded, "Over $200 for five books for five classes?"

Yes she replied, "and the books will cost you more the further along you get in college.

I wrote my check and headed back to the dorm. As soon as I got to my room,I called my mother and sobbed, "Mom, I've made a big mistake. College isn't for me. I want to come home."

In a kind voice, she responded, "Ellen, you're staying. College is where you need to be. I called my Mother, your Grandmother, and said the same thing. She gave me two pieces of advise: First, don't cry. You live closer to home than your roommate. If you're homesick, your roommate will get homesick to. And second, you are acting just like a girl who was in college with me. When this girl asked to come home after just moving into her dorm room, her parents packed up all her belongings and moved her back home. The girl is still living with her parents some twenty-five years later. Ellen, you're not like this girl. Your now independent; you can't turn back."

I turned the portable telephone off and thought, "If I could learn how to share, plane the classes I should take, and survive the college bookstore, then I could handle anything that lie ahead. College was wear I did need to be."

I laid the telephone down, dashed through the conecting bathroom, to ask my new freinds, "Does anyone want to ate microwave popcorn and watch the afternoon soaps with me?"

I tucked my mother's words away safely in my heart. I new I would do just find at brevard collage.

3.9 Editing

Editing is the stage after revising in which *correct grammar, sentence style, diction, punctuation,* and *spelling* are inspected. When editing a paper, focus attention not on the concepts, content, or logic, but on the clarity of sentences and the correctness of the grammar. If problems of organization and logic still exist, *revise* the paper more before *editing.* Editing should be strictly for grammar and individual sentence structure.

Problem Solving Example:

 Your professor asks you to edit your paper. He wants you to look for errors in grammar, sentence style, punctuation, and spelling. How might your edited paper look?

 Below is how your edited paper might look. Corrections that were made are in boldface. Note that this is not the final copy. You will be making more corrections in the next stage, proofreading.

Adapting to College Life

My life changed when I went to Brevard college. I had to learn to be **independent**. At home, I had my own room and bath, and I could go to my parents for advice. Now, at college, I had a **roommate**, shared a bathroom with 3 other people, and no one to depend on but myself.

Learning to share a living space was hard. At my home in North **Carolina**, I had my own bedroom. Now, I was sharing a dormitory room with a girl from New Jersey. My roommate and I spent over two hours discussing who should get what bed, **dresser**, closet, book **shelves** and desk.

Next, came the bathroom. At home, I had my own private bathroom, and I could spread out my shampoo and cosmetics all over the vanity. Now, my bathroom connected to the next dormitory room, and I shared it with my roommate and the two girls in the next room. The four of us had to decide on a **morning** bathroom schedule based upon who had the earlier class, and we had to devise a **weekly** bathroom cleaning schedule. We each had to carry our toiletries to and from the bathroom in a plastic pail. It took me several weeks to adjust to sharing my living space and my bathroom.

If I had a problem, I could no longer go to my **parents**. Instead, I had an advisor to handle it. My advisor was an instructor in the Department of **English**. He is an older gentlemen, who spoke more like a grandfather than a stranger. In his office, he had a Boston rocker. At our first meeting, he told me to sit in the chair, and said, **"Ellen**, rocking will make you less nervous. He helped me to decide what courses to take as well as how to read the college's schedule. He went on to say the required course for freshmen, College Survival Skills, would help me with my adjust to college life. He logged my registration for College Survival Skills into his computer. Then, we discussed what other courses I should take. We agreed on western civilization, freshman composition I, calculus, and **Japanese** I, which he keyed into his computer. When he was done he handed me a copy of my schedule and said, "Come by as often as often as you like. Remember, I am here to help you."

Afterwards, I had to go to the bookstore to purchase my books. The bookstore was huge and crowded with students. It looked like a big department store at the mall. Instead of **clothes** and accessories, it had **aisles** and **aisles** of books for every subject being offered at the college. It took me over two hours to find my books. I got lost in the aisles and ended up in the medical school section when I searched for the textbook for my Japanese class. **A** medical **school** student had to point me to the textbook for my Japanese class. After finding my books, I went to the cashier. After she scanned the bar code on each book, she said, "honey, that will be $260.50."

I responded, "Over $200 for five books for five classes?"

Yes she replied, "and the books will cost you more the further along you get in college.

I wrote my check and headed back to the dorm. As soon as I got to my room, I called my mother and sobbed, "Mom, I've made a big mistake. College isn't for me. I want to come home."

In a kind voice, she responded, "Ellen, you're staying. College is where you need to be. I called my my **mother**, your **grandmother**, and said the same thing. She gave me two **pieces** of **advice**: First, don't cry. You live closer to home than your roommate. If you're homesick, your roommate will get homesick to. And second, you're acting just like a girl who was in college with me. When this girl asked to come home after just moving into her dorm room, her parents packed up all her belongings and moved her back home. The girl is still living with her parents some twenty-five years later. **Ellen**, you're not like this girl. You're now independent; you can't turn back."

I turned the portable telephone off and thought, "if I could learn how to share, plane the classes I should take, and survive the college bookstore, then I could handle anything that lie ahead. College was wear I did need to be."

I laid the telephone down, dashed through the **connecting** bathroom, to ask my new **friends**, "Does anyone want to **eat** microwave popcorn and watch the afternoon soaps with me?"

I tucked my mother's words away safely in my heart. I **knew** I would do just find at brevard **college**.

3.10 Proofreading

Proofreading is the next to last stage of the writing process. In this stage, check the paper for mechanical errors such as doubled words, mistyped words *(typos)*, incorrect margins, or unwanted marks of any kind. In proofreading, the goal is to "clean up" the document so that it has no typing or visual errors and is ready for the reader's eye.

PROOFREADERS' MARKS

Mark Made in Margin	Explanation	How Indicated in the Copy
1. Marks of Instruction		
ℒ	delete, take out	She sold the book.
sold ^	insert	She ^ the book.
⑤Ⓟ	spell out	She sold ⑩ copies.

1. Marks of Instruction (continued)

  transpose She the sold book.

⁊ paragraph ... read. She sold the book.

(Run-in) run together read.
  She sold the book.

new line new line She sold books in Paris, NY

stet leave as it stands She sold the book.

ꙅ// Use slash to separate proofreading symbols and to indicate number of repetitions She sold the book pens and pencils.

2. Marks Regarding Type Style

(ital) set in *italics* She sold the book.

(bf) set in boldface She sold the book.

(ul) underline She sold 10 copies.

ROM change from *italic* to roman She sold the book.

cap set in Capitals she sold the book.

l.c. set in lowercase She Sold the Book.

u/l set in upper and lowercase SHE SOLD THE BOOK.

ⓢⓒ	set in SMALL CAPS	She sold the book.
\3/	superscript	xy³/
/2\	subscript	H₂O

3. Marks Regarding Defects in Type

broken
type | broken letters | She sold the book.

w.f. | wrong font | She sold the book.

‖ | align vertically | She sold the book.
He sold the book, too.

═ | align horizontally | she sold the book.

4. Marks Regarding Spacing

⌒ | close up | She s old the book.

⸗ | delete and close up | She sold the book.

| insert space | She sold the book.

⮫ | indent | ⮫ She sold the book.

⌐ ⌐ | center | STUPID PET TRICKS
1. The Froggy Broad Jump
2. Cat Ventriloquism

⌐ | move left as indicated | She sold the book.

⌐ | move right as indicated | She sold the book.

⌐ | raise as indicated | She sold the book.

4. Marks Regarding Spacing (continued)

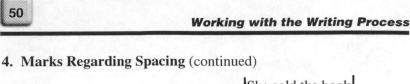

	lower as indicated	She sold the book

eq   correct spacing between letters   She sold the book.

leading   correct spacing between between lines   She sold the book. He read the book she wrote.

5. Marks of Punctuation

⊙   period   She sold the book

⌒   comma   She sold the book and went on her way.

semicolon   She sold the book she always manages to sell books.

colon   For example ten books, four tapes ...

apostrophe   It is the author's copy.

open and closed quotes   She said: Forget what you have to do.

exclamation point   Stop the presses.

question mark.   Did they stop the presses

⊜   equal sign   SILENCE -DEATH

‗	hyphen	He generated a printout. ^
$\frac{1}{N}$	one-en dash	Pages 2, 5, and 26 89 are ^ ruined
$\frac{1}{M}$	one-em dash	She went with the book. ^
‹/›	open and close parentheses	She Lisa sold the book. ^ ^
‹/›	open and close brackets	She selled *sic* the book. ^ ^

Problem Solving Example:

Q Your professor asks you to proofread your paper. What marks would you make in the paper?

A Below is how your proofreading might look.

<u>Adapting to College Life</u> (bf)

My life changed when I went to Brevard College. I had to learn to be independent. At home, I had my own room and bath, and I could go to my parents for advice. Now, at college, I had a roommate, shared a bathroom with (3) other people, and no one to depend on but myself. (sp)

 Learning to share a living space was hard.   At my home in North Carolina, I had my own bedroom.   Now, I was sharing a dormitory room with a girl from New Jersey. My roommate and I spent over two hours discussing who should get what bed, dresser, closet, book shelves and desk.

Next, came the bathroom. AT HOME, I had my own private bath- ull room, and I could spread out my shampoo and cosmetics all over the vanity. Now, my bathroom connected to the next dormitory room, and stet I shared it with my roommate and the two girls in the next room. The four of us had to decide on a morning bathroom schedule based upon who had the earlier class, and we had to devise a weekly bathroom cleaning schedule. We each had to carry our toiletries to and from the 9 bathroom in a plastic pail. It took me several weeks to adjust to sharing my living space and my bathroom.

If I had a problem, I could no longer go to my parents. Instead, I had an advisor to handle it. My advisor was an instructor in the Department of English. He was an older gentleman who spoke more like a grandfather than a stranger. In his office, he had a Boston rocker. At our first meeting, he told me to sit in the chair, and said, " Ellen, rocking will make you less nervous." He helped me to decide what courses to take as well as how to read the college's schedule. He went on to say that the required course for freshmen, College Survival Skills, would help me ment with my adjust to college life. He logged my registration for College Survival Skills into his computer. Then, we discussed what other courses I should take. We agreed on Western Civilization, Freshman Composition I, Calculus, and Japanese I, which he logged into his computer. When # he was done, he handed me a copy of my schedule and said, "Come by as often as often as you like. Remember, I am here to help you.

Afterwards, I had to go to the bookstore to purchase my books. The bookstore was huge and crowded with students. It looked like a big department store at the mall. Instead of *clothes and accessories* it w.f. had aisles and aisles of books for every subject being offered at the college. It took me over two hours to find my books. I got lost in the aisles and ended up in the anatomy section when I searched for the textbook for my Japanese class. An upper classman had to point me to the textbook for my Japanese class. After finding my books, I went to the cashier. After she scanned the bar code on each book, she said, "honey, that will be $260.50."

I responded, "Over $200 for five books for five classes?"

"Yes," she replied, "and the books will cost you more the further along you get in college." *leading*

I wrote my check and headed back to the dorm. As soon as I got to my room, I called my mother and sobbed, "Mom, I've made a big mistake. College isn't for me. I want to come home." ¶ #

In a kind voice, she responded, "Ellen, you're staying. College is where you need to be. I called my ~~my~~ mother, your grandmother, and said the same thing. She gave me two pieces of advice: First, don't cry. You live closer to home than your roommate. If you're homesick, your roommate will get homesick too. And second, you're acting just like a girl who was in college with me. When this girl asked to come home after just moving into her dorm room, her parents packed up all her belongings and moved her back home. The girl is still living with her parents some twenty-five years later. Ellen, you're not like this girl. You're now independent you can't turn back."

I turned the portable telephone off and thought, "If I could learn how to share, plan the classes I should take, and survive the college bookstore, then I could handle anything that lay ahead. College (was) where I did need to be." *ital*

I laid the telephone down, dashed through the connecting bathroom, to ask my new friends, "Does anyone want to eat microwave popcorn and watch the afternoon soaps with me." ?/

I tucked my mother's words away safely in my heart. I knew I would do just fine at Brevard College.

3.11 Final Copy

After all these stages have been completed, typed, or finished, print the final copy with the proofreading changes included so that the paper is turned in as a clean copy, with absolutely no errors.

Problem Solving Example:

Your professor asks you to turn in your final copy. How might your final draft look?

Below is how your final draft might look.

Adapting to College Life

My life changed when I went to Brevard College. I had to learn to be independent. At home, I had my own room and bath, and I could go to my parents for advice. Now, at college, I had a roommate, shared a bathroom with three other people, and had no one to depend on but myself.

Learning to share a living space was hard. At my home in North Carolina, I had my own bedroom. Now, I was sharing a dormitory room with a girl from New Jersey. My roommate and I spent over two hours discussing who should get which bed, dresser, closet, book shelves and desk.

Next came the bathroom. At home, I had my own private bathroom, and I could spread out my shampoo and cosmetics all over the vanity. Now, my bathroom connected to the next dormitory room, and I shared it with my roommate and the two girls in the next room. The four of us had to decide on a morning bathroom schedule based upon who had the earliest class, and we had to devise a weekly bathroom cleaning schedule. We each had to carry our toiletries to and from the bathroom in a plastic pail. It took me several weeks to adjust to sharing my living space and my bathroom.

If I had a problem, I could no longer go to my parents. Instead, I had an advisor to handle it. My advisor was an instructor in the Department of English. He was an older gentleman who spoke more like a grandfather than a stranger. In his office, he had a Boston rocker. At our first meeting, he told me to sit in the chair, and said, "Ellen, rocking will make you less nervous." He helped me to decide what courses to take as well as how to read the college's schedule. He went on to say that the required course for freshmen, College Survival Skills, would help me with my adjustment to college life. He logged my registration for College Survival Skills into his computer. Then, we discussed what other courses I should take. We agreed on Western Civilization, Freshman Composition I, Calculus, and Japanese I, which he logged into his computer. When he was done, he handed me a copy of my schedule and said, "Come by as often as often as you like. Remember, I am here to help you."

Afterwards, I had to go to the bookstore to purchase my books. The bookstore was huge and crowded with students. It looked like a big department store at the mall. Instead of clothes and accessories, it had aisles and aisles of books for every subject being offered at the college. It took me over two hours to find my books. When I searched for the textbook for my Japanese class I got lost in the aisles and ended up in the anatomy section. An upper classman had to point me to the textbook for my Japanese class. After finding my books, I went to the cashier. She scanned the bar code on each book and said, "Honey, that will be $260.50."

I responded, "Over $200 for five books for five classes?"

"Yes," she replied, "and the books will cost you more the further along you get in college."

I wrote my check and headed back to the dorm. As soon as I got to my room, I called my mother and sobbed, "Mom, I've made a big mistake. College isn't for me. I want to come home.

In a kind voice, she responded, "Ellen, you're staying. College is where you need to be. When I was your age, I had called my mother, your grandmother, and said the same thing. She gave me two pieces of advice. First, don't cry. You live closer to home than your roommate. If you're homesick, your roommate will get homesick too. And second, you're acting just like a girl who was in college with me. When this girl asked to come home after just moving into her dorm room, her parents packed up all her belongings and moved her back home. The girl is still living with her parents some twenty-five years later. Ellen, you're not like this girl. You're independent now; you can't turn back."

I turned off the portable telephone and thought, "If I could learn how to share, plan the classes I should take, and survive the college bookstore, then I could handle anything that lay ahead. College *was* where I needed to be."

I laid the telephone down and dashed through the connecting bathroom to ask my new friends, "Does anyone want to eat microwave popcorn and watch the afternoon soaps with me?"

I tucked my mother's words away safely in my heart.   I knew I would do just fine at Brevard College.

Quiz: Introduction – Working with the Writing Process

Questions 1-10 are based on the following passage. Read the passage carefully before choosing your answers.

THE Number of the Souls in Ireland being usually reckoned one Million and a half; of these I calculate there may be about Two hundred Thousand Couple whose Wives are Breeders; from which Number I subtract thirty thousand Couples, who are able to maintain their own Children; although I apprehend
5 there cannot be so many, under *the present Distresses of the Kingdom;* but this being granted, there will remain an Hundred and Seventy Thousand Breeders. I again subtract Fifty Thousand, for those Women who miscarry, or whose Children die by Accident, or Disease, within the Year. There only remain an Hundred and Twenty Thousand Children of poor Parents, annually born:
10 The Question therefore is, How this Number shall be reared, and provided for? Which, as I have already said, under the present Situation of Affairs, is utterly impossible, by all the Methods hitherto proposed: For we can *neither employ them in Handicraft* or *Agriculture,* we neither build Houses, (I mean in the Country) nor cultivate Land: They can very seldom pick up a Livelyhood
15 by *Stealing* until they arrive at six Years old; except where they are of towardly Parts; although, I confess, they learn the Rudiments much earlier; during which Time, they can, however, be properly looked upon only as Probationers; as I have been informed by a principal Gentleman in the Country of *Cavan,* who protested to me, that he never knew above one or two Instances under the
20 Age of six, even in a Part of the Kingdom *so renowned for the quickest Proficiency in that Art.*
I AM assured by our Merchants, that a Boy or a Girl before twelve Years old, is no saleable Commodity; and even when they come to this Age, they will not yield above Three Pounds, or Three Pounds and a half a Crown at most, on

25 the Exchange; which cannot turn to Account either to the Parents or the Kingdom; the Charge of Nutriment and Rags, having been at least four Times that Value.

I SHALL now therefore humbly propose my own Thoughts, which I hope will not be liable to the least Objection.

30 I HAVE been assured by a very knowing *American* of my Acquaintance in *London;* that a young healthy Child, well nursed, is, at a Year old, a most delicious, nourishing, and wholesome Food; whether *Stewed, Roasted, Baked,* or *Boiled;* and, I make no doubt, that it will equally serve in a *Fricasie,* or *Ragoust.*

35 I DO therefore humbly offer it to *publick Consideration,* that of the Hundred and Twenty Thousand Children, already computed, Twenty thousand may be reserved for Breed; whereof only one Fourth Part to be Males; which is more than we allow to *Sheep, black Cattle,* or *Swine,* and my Reason is, that these Children are seldom the Fruits of Marriage, *a Circumstance not much regarded by*
40 *our Savages;* therefore, *one Male* will be sufficient to serve *four Females.* That the remaining Hundred thousand, may, at a Year old, be offered in *Sale to the Persons of Quality* and *Fortune,* through the Kingdom; always advising the Mother to let them suck plentifully in the last Month, so as to render them plump, and fat for a good Table. A child will make two Dishes at an Entertainment for
45 Friends; and when the Family dines alone, the fore or hind Quarter will make a reasonable Dish; and seasoned with a little Pepper and Salt, will be very good Boiled on the fourth Day, especially in the *Winter.*

I HAVE reckoned upon a Medium, that a Child just born will weigh Twelve Pounds; and in a solar Year, if tolerably nursed, encreaseth to twenty
50 eight Pounds.

I GRANT this Food will be somewhat dear, and therefore *very proper for Landlords;* who, as they have already devoured most of the Parents, seem to have the best Title to the Children.

INFANTS Flesh will be in Season throughout the Year; but more plentiful
55 in *March,* and a little before and after: For we are told by a grave Author, an eminent *French* Physician, that *Fish being a prolifick Dyet,* there are more Children born in *Roman Catholick Countries* about Nine Months after Lent than at any other Season: Therefore reckoning a Year after Lent, the Markets will be more glutted than usual; because the Number of *Popish Infants,* is, at
60 least three to one in this Kingdom; and therefore it will have one other Collateral Advantage, by lessening the Number of *Papists* among us.

I HAVE already computed the Charge of nursing a Beggar's Child (in which List I reckon all *Cottagers, Labourers,* and Four fifths of the *Farmers*) to be about two Shillings *per Annum,* Rags included: and I believe, no Gentleman
65 would repine to give Ten Shillings for the *Carcase of a good fat Child;* which, as I have said, will make four Dishes of excellent nutritive Meat, when he hath only some particular Friend, or his own Family, to dine with him. Thus the Squire will learn to be a good Landlord, and grow popular among his Tenants; the mother will have Eight Shillings net Profit, and be fit for Work until she
70 produceth another Child.

1.   The phrase "I GRANT this Food will be somewhat dear, and there- fore *very proper for Landlords,* who, as they have already de- voured most of the Parents, seem to have the best Title to the Children" does all of the following EXCEPT

     (A)   understands the cost of the "Food."

     (B)   reverses the metaphor which dominates the passage.

     (C)   sarcastically indicts the children's parents.

     (D)   reveals the speaker's attitudes toward landlords and tenants in a seeming aside.

     (E)   suggests persons who may play a role in giving the children better lives.

2.   Throughout the passage, poor children and their parents are meta- phorically described using images of

     (A)   urban decay.

     (B)   animal husbandry.

     (C)   business transactions.

     (D)   scientific analysis.

     (E)   religious rituals.

3.   What does the word "popish" (line 59) mean?

    (A) tiny

    (B) unruly

    (C) Roman Catholic

    (D) fish eating

    (E) Irish

4.   What effect does the construction of the argument in lines 1-47 have upon the reader?

    (A) Its seemingly rational progression makes the startling proposal even more jarring.

    (B) The emphasis upon "Souls" (line1) initiates an atmosphere of religious reverence.

    (C) The references to animal breeding in the first and fifth paragraphs detract from the passage's main point.

    (D) The use of census-like statistics before the proposal confuses the issue and makes the reader more suseptible to persuasion.

    (E) The emphatic first person opening of each paragraph except the first underscores the speaker's reasonableness.

5.   The antecedent of "many" (line 5) is

    (A) "Children" (line 4).

    (B) "Number" (line 3).

    (C) "Souls" (line 1).

    (D) "Wives" (line 3).

    (E) "Couples" (line 4).

6. Which of the following can be inferred to be the intent of the passage?

    I.   To rebuke landlords for their callousness

    II.   To force a reexamination of other proposals

    III. To offer a measured solution to a crisis

    IV.   To build the speaker's reputation as a civic-minded person

    (A) I only

    (B) I and II only

    (C) III and IV only

    (D) I, II, and III only

    (E) I, II, III, and IV

7. Stylistically, the passage may be best described as

    (A) philosophical.

    (B) lyrical.

    (C) scientific.

    (D) hortative.

    (E) satirical.

8. The speaker's use of "Breeders" (line 3) as a predicate adjective for "Wives"

    (A) depersonalizes the women.

    (B) praises the women's fertility.

    (C) describes the women's occupation.

    (D) distinguishes the women from the men.

    (E) criticizes the women for having children.

9. The phrase "I SHALL now therefore humbly propose my own Thoughts, which I hope will not be liable to the least Objection" (lines 28-29) is an example of

    A) hyperbole.

    (B) oxymoron.

    (C) understatement.

    (D) metaphor.

    (E) digression.

10. In the context of the passage as a whole, the references to women as "Breeders" and children as a "saleable Commodity" (line 23) serve as

    (A) digressions from the course of the arguments.

    (B) statements of fact.

    (C) summaries of the argument.

    (D) omens of the proposal to come.

    (E) objections to the proposal itself.

ANSWER KEY

1.	(C)	6.	(B)
2.	(B)	7.	(E)
3.	(C)	8.	(A)
4.	(A)	9.	(C)
5.	(E)	10.	(D)

CHAPTER 4

Types of Papers in Basic Composition

4.1 Euclid and the Logic of Basic Composition

Most college writing instructors require essays to be written in several forms, serving various logical and informational purposes (see Chapter 2 for a discussion of purposes in writing and reading). This chapter reviews the essential forms for writing and the purposes they serve. First, however, the basic logical format for compositions in English need to be reviewed. This format dates back to ancient Greece, Euclid, and geometry.

High school geometry class and Euclid's theorems aid in the understanding of why essays must have three basic parts: (1) the introduction, (2) the body, or development section, and (3) the conclusion. Euclid's theorems represent a basic logical form: (1) the idea to be proved, (2) the demonstration of the reasoning behind the proof, and (3) a statement showing that the proof demonstrated that the idea is true: "Q.E.D." (thus it is demonstrated). In an analogous manner, the logic of composition follows the same route. Just as in the opening of Euclid's theorems, a good essay in English will have an introduction which states, directly or indirectly, a main point or thesis that the writer sets out to demonstrate or prove.

The middle part of an essay, like the "proofs" in Euclid's theorems, is the *body of the essay,* or a *set of paragraphs following the introduction that supports the main point or thesis of the essay with evidence.* In Euclid's case, for example, when he tries to prove that "the sum of the interior angles of any triangle always equals 180 degrees" he uses the middle part of his proof to demonstrate that the angles of every major case of a triangle (isosceles, right, and obtuse), no matter how big or small, always add up to 180°. In the end, he *concludes* by saying: "Q.E.D.," or roughly, "Thus it is demonstrated." Similarly, essays in English, if not narratives that show a course of events in time or space, employ this same pattern. Writers use an *introduction, body,* and *conclusion* to show (1) a statement of his or her topic and what the main point is, (2) support and proof of the thesis, and (3) a reminder to the reader of the position, or thesis, sometimes including a recommendation or action that might be taken in the future.

4.1.1 Purposes in Academic Writing

The purposes for writing in college English are the same as those for reading (see Chapter 2 for more detail on the purposes of reading). However, in writing, essays take the shape they do because they serve a particular logical purpose. Professors may ask students to write an essay with a particular purpose, in which case the essay takes shape to suit that purpose. The fundamental purposes in writing in college English are (1) *to express,* (2) *to describe,* (3) *to explain,* (4) *to inform,* and (5) *to persuade (or convince)* in order to make an audience aware of a particular idea or topic.

A sixth purpose that doesn't often show up in college English is *entertaining.* A writer may write an essay with no particular concern to prove anything, but to make the readers laugh, wonder, or marvel at some phenomenon, idea, event, or person. Using humor in an essay may be a subtle technique for persuading an audience to a particular point of view; however, this method of persuasion does not employ reason, but simply makes the reader feel good about the idea.

Another form of persuasion, called *propaganda,* uses emotions and psychological ploys rather than logic to convince a reader to accept a course of action or belief. Television commercials are the most common form of propaganda that is seen daily.

Every essay must be written with the knowledge that someone else will read it. This reading audience must be considered when writing essays. Consequently, different essays use different kinds of *narration,* or ways of telling, to achieve their differing purposes. These purposes for writing, which are described and explained below, form a hierarchy of increasing complexity, from the simplest to the most complex purposes and writing tasks. This chart reflects such a hierarchy.

HIERARCHY OF VALIDITY OF PURPOSE

Most Logically	Persuading
Complex	Informing
	Explaining
	Describing
Simplest	Expressing

In the chart, each purpose logically supports the one above it. Essays in which persuasion is the primary purpose may or will subordinate and use all the other purposes in *argumentation* to convince a reader or prove a point. For example, to prove that Corvettes are better than Ferraris as sports cars, the writer would necessarily have to describe both cars and the difference between them.

All essay writing informs readers in some sense, but a persuasive writer should use descriptive and explanatory techniques in his/her essay—in this case, concerning Corvettes and Ferraris, to inform the audience of particularly important differences relevant to his or her thesis. Finally, the writer who tries to persuade uses this information in order to convince the audience of the validity or truth of the thesis he or she proposes. In other words, persuasion is the "principal" of all purposes in the "school" of writing, and all the other purposes are "assistant principals," so to speak. They can each be the main purpose of an essay, but as the responsibility of the writer moves from reporting (describing, explaining, and informing) to convincing, more and more skills and secondary purposes need to be utilized by the writer. Instructors usually teach this writing hierarchy to students.

4.1.2   Introduction, Body and Conclusion

The formal parts (sections) of most academic essays include the *introduction,* the *body* or *development,* and the *conclusion.* In addition to knowing the format of the essay, students should know that these sections of essays vary in intent and content. Fundamentally, there are eight typical ways to introduce a subject, several techniques to control the developmental section, and various ways to conclude the essay. How this is done is dependent on the purpose of the paper.

The introduction allows the writer to *present the topic and state precisely what the writer wants to say about the topic.* The writer should then move into a close supportive discussion of the main point in the middle paragraphs. Many writers suggest that the paper/essay be presented in the following way:

THE ACADEMIC/TECHNICAL PYRAMID
A Common Organizational Pattern

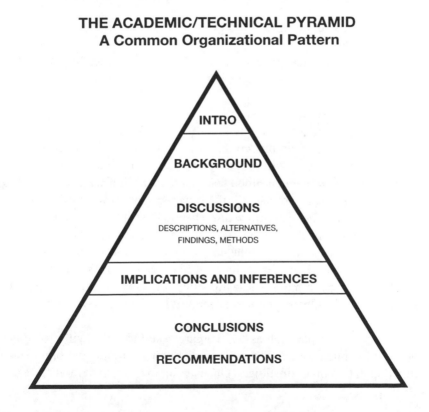

INTRO

BACKGROUND

DISCUSSIONS

DESCRIPTIONS, ALTERNATIVES, FINDINGS, METHODS

IMPLICATIONS AND INFERENCES

CONCLUSIONS

RECOMMENDATIONS

There are *eight standard ways to introduce a topic,* though others are possible. Make note of the possibilities listed below:

1. Start with an interesting fact, related to the thesis, that catches the reader's attention.

2. Use an anecdote from personal experience or personal knowledge that sets up the situation or illustrates the thesis.

3. Use a quotation relevant to the thesis from a leading authority or related figure in the news.

4. Use some compelling remark to pull the reader into the essay.

5. Begin with a question that the essay can answer.

6. Start with an illustration of the problem or situation.

7. Start with general information about the topic leading down to the thesis statement as the last sentence of the opening paragraph.

8. Boldly state the thesis.

The middle paragraphs contain the *body,* or *development* of the essay. In college, you will probably only encounter very short essays (of around 500 words) on timed tests such as mid-terms and finals. In such an essay, there are usually three paragraphs in which the writer brings up the *evidence* or *information* needed to support the main point or thesis stated in the first paragraph. The *body* uses *transitions,* or words and phrases that move the *narration* or *narrator's voice* forward along with the logical development of his or her ideas (such as "however" and "for example"). These transitions develop the flow of thought for the reader while deepening the support for the thesis or main point.

For the most part, the essays you are asked to write will probably need to be much longer and will involve more complicated organization depending on their subject. Once again, in order to demonstrate as clearly as possible the principles involved in writing various types of essays, the sample essays in this book will be quite succinct. You should understand that, were they for an actual college course, they would probably need to be expanded.

The conclusion for a given essay serves two purposes: (1) to provide a resolution or closure for the logical development of the essay, and (2) to offer the reader a sense of ending to the discussion at hand—in other words, the *conclusion,* as in the introduction and body, has a *rhetorical* as well as *logical* purpose. The *rhetorical* purpose deals with the reader's expectations and resolves them to create the sense of an ending or beginning. The *logical* purpose is that which resolves the reader's need for a sensible ending to the thought developed in the essay. There are *several ways to conclude an essay.* Make note of the list below:

1.   Rephrase the thesis in light of the whole discussion, or create a Euclidian equation as described in the introduction.

2.   Encourage a change of action, or a next step to follow through with the idea.

3.   Point the reader in the direction of larger issues that might relate to the thesis.

4.   Summarize the main points the essay covered.

4.2   Point of View: Narrative in the First Person or Third Person

Essays in college English are commonly *narrated,* or *told to the reader,* from one of two basic *points of view,* or perspectives. These perspectives can be either personal or objective: *first person* or *third person,* and are called *points of view. First person* is the use of "I," "me," "we," and other first-person pronouns to speak to the reader from the page using the "I"/"You" relationship. For example, autobiographies often use the first person point of view to discuss the course of the writer's life.

An autobiography would sound something like this:

> "I was born in the state of Kentucky in a small cabin near
> the river we called Muddy River in 1765. I was the last son
> of Irish immigrants from County Cork."

The *first person* addresses the reader directly. This *point of view* is usually associated and used with personal essays that tell stories to make a point. The *third person* narrative is so called because the narrator does not use "I" and "you" as if in a personal conversation with the reader, but the third persons of the conjugation of the verb, "it" and "they," to discuss a topic from a more distant perspective. The third person would not say "I think that pollution is bad for people ... ," but rather, "Pollution (or 'it') is bad for people." Thus, in the example above, if the book was changed from an autobiography to a biography of someone about whom the author is writing, it would be written in the third person and sound something like this:

> "John Smith (or 'He') was born in the state of Kentucky in
> a small cabin near the river the pioneers (or 'they') called
> Muddy River in 1765. He was the last son of Irish immi-
> grants from County Cork."

The "I's" change to the person's name or to the third person pronoun, "he" or "she." Things change to "it" for "river," if that is the thing, or to the name of the object that the writer is addressing. Using this third person point of view should be intentional, and, because it sounds more objective, third person puts the emphasis on the topic rather than the narrator's personal view of the topic. Consequently, professors will make an effort to move college writers away from the first person *(personal)* to the third person *(objective)*. Remember, never shift the point of view in the middle of an essay or paper.

4.3   Patterns of Organization

Writers use several types of organizational patterns in their writing. These patterns break down into two sections called *natural* and *logical*.

The writer employs *natural patterns* of organization most often, but not exclusively, in essays which use the first person point of view to express, describe, or explain. Essays of personal opinion or memory almost always use natural patterns. *Logical patterns* of organization are most often, but not exclusively, used in essays which use the third person point of view and whose purposes are to explain, inform, or persuade.

4.3.1 Chronological and Spatial Patterns of Organization

The two patterns of natural organization, *chronological* and *spatial,* come from the way in which people *naturally* view the world: in the order of time unfolding forward, or in a change from one space to another. Since these patterns of organization reflect the natural order of the world, they are the most natural to write. Children, for example, can tell a story in this way long before they can give logical reasons for their behavior in the story they tell.

In an essay organized *chronologically,* one event happens after another just the way it did or will in time:

> "In 1980, I began working on the railroad. ... In 1984, the railroad went bankrupt, so I went to work with the bus companies in New York. ... By the time 1990 came around, I had my own bus company, and I was making a real living as the owner of a statewide fleet of buses employing over 200 people."

The writer writes about one thing after another because that is the *order in which these things happened in time.* This is chronological organization.

In *spatially organized essays,* one paragraph follows another based on *a planned sequential change in the place of the events or action.* Also, this pattern usually uses considerable description. Look at how the passage above changes when space (location), not time, control the sequence of discussion:

> "In Chicago, I began working on the railroad. ... The railroad went bankrupt in that city, so I went to work with the

bus companies in New York. ... New York was too competitive, so I took my family to the smaller town of Burlington, Vermont. ... There, I started my own bus company, and I was soon making a real living as the owner of a statewide fleet of buses employing over 200 people."

Chronological and spatial patterns of organization are often combined, with one or the other dominating the narrative sequence. Thus, if the two patterns were combined based on the examples above, and if time rather than space dominates the narrative sequence, it would sound like this:

"In 1980, I began working on the railroad in Chicago. ... In 1984, the railroad went bankrupt, so I went to work with the bus companies in New York. ... By the time 1990 came around, I had my own bus company in Burlington, Vermont, and I was making a real living as the owner of a statewide fleet of buses employing over 200 people."

Description is a special case of chronological and spatial organization that *lets the reader know the aesthetic impact that the subject under description has on the senses of the observer, or writer, as relevant to the discussion.*

In the example of the railroad worker above, the passage could become much more vivid if the writer made an *appeal to the senses of the reader* by increasing the description of detail—details that increase the clarity with which the reader imagines seeing, hearing, tasting, touching, or smelling, the place and time the writer portrays.

"In 1980, I began working on the railroad in Chicago. The railroad buildings were made of crumbling brick and cement, and most of the windows in the stations were broken or painted over. The rails themselves were crooked, loose, and rusted over in more places than I care to remember. Pretty soon, I started to feel discouraged by all this ugliness and these badly maintained machines. ... In 1984, the railroad in Chicago went bankrupt, so I went to work with the bus companies in New York. The situation that greeted me in New York wasn't much better. If anything, it was worse. The platforms at the Port Authority bus terminal were covered with litter and dirt. The awful smell left behind by the helpless homeless, and the used drug paraphernalia lying on the tracks told a real story in itself. There were so many people in New York—from midgets to giants, from the pretty to the ugly, that you just felt overwhelmed. This, too, didn't seem like the place for me. ... By the time 1990 came around, I had my own bus company in Burlington, Vermont. Burlington was a beautiful country village town with clean streets and air that smelled like pure oxygen, if pure oxygen had a smell—fresh, clean, and unpolluted. Burlington was very different; here, at least, you couldn't see the air you breathed. Before long, I was making a real living as the owner of a statewide fleet of double-decker gold and gray buses, and I was employing over 200 people."

Notice all the words that appeal to the reader's sense of sight, touch, smell, and beauty, and the aesthetic impact in the enhanced passage. The writer often uses description in personal essays to enhance the effect on the reader and to liven up his or her topic of discussion. Powerful descriptions are often a major part of writers' personal journals. Keeping a journal is an excellent way to enhance descriptive skills.

4.3.2 Logical Patterns of Organization

Unlike spatial and chronological patterns of organization, *logical patterns* are organized not according to the natural patterns of time and place, but according to the patterns that arise out of reason. Euclid's order of thought in the theorems of plane geometry suggests a beginning, a middle, and an end (or introduction, middle development, and conclusion). In logically patterned essays a writer uses this same format.

In organizational patterns governed by the logic of the topic and thesis, the beginning, middle, and end are about one idea, focused and explained or developed to meet the needs of a logical situation. This logical situation ranges from *defining* some word, thing, or idea to using any, several, or all of the patterns of organization. Using this pattern along with any and all of the less complex purposes of writing allows a writer to use *argumentation* in order to persuade the reader to be for or against the topic under discussion.

This chart shows the hierarchy of patterns, moving from the simple to the complex, from the bottom to the top.

HIERARCHY OF PATTERNS

Least complex pattern

Definition

Process/Procedure Analysis

Comparison/Contrast

Classification Analysis

Problem/Solution

Causal Analysis

Most complex pattern

Argumentation

A writer may use any, several, or all of the patterns of organization on its or their own, or in differing combinations to write a good argument. The ability of the writer to manipulate these patterns of thought is the only thing that can limit the complexity of possible approaches he or she takes in proving a point or thesis. The patterns of organization are not arbitrary, but reflect the logical thinking and purpose that drives them. A comparative analysis is appropriate to an argumentative paper that attempts to convince its audience that one idea, object, or person is better or worse than another. The patterns arise out of a need to respond to the fundamental patterns of logical thinking.

4.4 Definition

Writing a *definition* is important because definitions are the bases of all arguments. A writer cannot argue about something if he or she or the reader does not understand the central terms. For example, in order to argue that "handsome is as handsome does," the writer first has to define what is meant by "handsome." An essay using the definition of a term as an organizational pattern seeks to argue for the nature of an abstraction (What is love? What is truth? What does it mean to be human?). Definitions can also be utilized for a more limited and technical purpose, such as to define a drill press by explaining and describing its physical and functioning parts. Essays that define are generally informational and instructional, rarely argumentative.

4.5 Process or Procedure Analysis

In a *process* or *procedure analysis,* the writer organizes his writing around the *necessary and essential order of a set of steps.* Some procedure analyses might argue that there is a best way to do something, while others only wish to explain what the process or procedure is in order to inform the reader. For example, a cook might explain the best steps to take to bake a cake, but a biologist would report and explain how the process of photosynthesis works in nature.

An instructor may require students to write a process analysis about a more simple topic. For example, professors might ask their students to write a step-by-step account of how to use the reference materials in the library to look up a book or to write a paper about how to put together a chair. In any event, the paper is called an *analysis.* In an analysis, *the writer breaks down a whole process or procedure into its important steps or segments. The paper should be instructional and informative.* The most common form of a process analysis in everyday life, though not an essay, is the set of instructions that comes with the new chair, desk, or children's toy that "requires some assembly."

4.6 Classification Analysis

In the case of a *classification analysis,* the writer organizes a paper to show the *categories* or *types* of a given phenomenon. An assignment might call for an essay about "the major ways in which people amuse themselves in the summertime." The writer could demonstrate that there are three major types of amusement for people in the summer: (1) recreation in nature, (2) recreation with other human beings, and (3) recreation with machines. In the end, the paper would consist of a description and explanation of the major kinds of activity people might engage in for summertime fun.

There are no "right" or "wrong" categories for things. It is up to the individual to decide how to categorize things when writing a paper this way. One writer might just as legitimately organize his or her summertime recreation activities into not three, but five different ways: (1) things to eat, (2) things to see, (3) things to hear, (4) things to smell, and (5) things to touch. The choice of categories is up to the individual writer.

The writer may use a classification analysis to explain or inform the reader for instructional purposes about some idea, object, or person, or to persuade a reader that a given set of categories or types is the correct one, not only that it exists. A writer may have a thesis that states, "There are only two types of people in the world: the givers and the takers." The paper would then attempt to convince the reader of the truth or validity of this thesis. On the other hand, a writer could write a classification analysis that explains and informs the reader of the types and characteristics of the major classes of purebred dogs about which there are documented facts: (1) working dogs, (2) sporting dogs, and (3) show dogs. Thus, one can write a classification analysis that is a matter of opinion or one that is a matter of fact.

4.7 Causal Analysis

A *causal analysis* is rigorous and exacting. A *causal analysis* is actually a specialized form of a classification analysis in which the classification is always that of differing causes for the appearance or incidence of a phenomenon. This organizational pattern is driven by the answers to questions about why or why not something occurs. Look at the question, "Why do people travel?". To answer this question, the writer would examine possible reasons that people would travel.

A good causal analysis distinguishes between *trivial* and *important* causes for a given phenomenon. Readers are not interested in flippant or ridiculous reasons for something occurring, unless the reasons are part of a humorous essay whose purpose is entertainment, not instruction. For example, a trivial cause for why people travel might be that they like ice cream. First, this reason doesn't apply to all people who travel—not everyone likes ice cream—but, also there are far more important, fundamental, and universal reasons why people travel than the desire for ice cream. That people travel to secure sustenance and nutrition is a more substantial reason for travel.

A well-written causal analysis distinguishes between the two fundamental forms of causes: *the proximate* or immediate cause, and the *remote* or more distant or previous source for the occurrence of the phenomenon. Thus, the *proximate* cause for a car starting might be your turning the key in the ignition with the gears in "park." However, the *remote* cause is that a team of engineers and electricians put together the mechanical and electrical components of the engine and electrical system in such a way that, when the ignition key is turned with the car in "park," a process between gas and electricity called internal combustion creates a force that makes the engine run and keep on running. Similarly, one proximate cause for World War II in America was the Japanese attack on Pearl Harbor in 1941. One important remote cause, however, was the need for Japanese leaders to expand their empire in order to satisfy the growing energy needs of their increasingly powerful and demanding industrial economy.

A good causal analysis will also demonstrate and explain the important *types of causes* that may make something occur. In looking at the question, "Why do people travel?" the possible causes could be broken down into several critical areas: *physical, psychological, social, economic, political, geographical, intellectual,* and *aesthetic.* Other categories might come to mind while writing the essay (scientific, spiritual, etc.), but this set of categories will cover the territory in terms of what the writer needs to consider. Each of these categorical causes may be proximate and/or remote.

The proximate physical cause for a person to travel somewhere might be that he or she was asked to meet a friend at the store; the remote cause might be that the person wants to maintain the friendship he or she has with the person he or she is meeting. Just as a writer may explain and inform an audience of a phenomenon in nature that is unchangeable or argue for the validity of one explanation over another through all the other patterns of organization, he may do so through the use of the causal analysis.

Problem Solving Example:

Q   Television often causes viewers to lose touch with reality and become completely passive and unaware. Like other addictions, television provides a pleasurable escape route from action to inaction. Do you agree or disagree with this statement? Support your opinion with specific examples from history, current events, literature, or personal experience.

A   This Answer provides three sample essays which represent possible responses to the essay topic. Compare your own response to those given on the next few pages. Allow the strengths and weaknesses of the sample essays to help you to critique your own essay and improve your writing skills.

SAMPLE ESSAY: Well-written

In the past thirty years, television has become a very popular pastime for almost everyone. From the time the mother places the baby in his jumpseat in front of the television so that she can relax and have a second cup of coffee until the time the senior citizen in the retirement home watches Vanna White turn the letters on "Wheel of Fortune," Americans spend endless hours in front of the "boob tube." I believe that television can become an addiction that provides an escape from the problems of the world and from facing responsibility for your own life.

When my mother was a little girl, what did children do to entertain themselves? They played. Their games usually involved social interaction with other children as well as imaginatively creating entertainment for themselves. They also developed hobbies like woodworking and sewing. Today, few children really know how to play with each other or entertain themselves. Instead, they sit in front of the television, glued to cartoons that are senseless and often violent. Even if they watch educational programs like "Sesame Street," they don't really have to do anything but watch and listen to what the answer to the question is.

Teenagers, also, use television as a way of avoiding doing things that will help them mature. How many kids do much homework anymore? Why not? Because they come home from school tired and relax in front of the television. Even if they watch a controversial program about some problem in the world like AIDS or the war in the Middle East, they don't usually do anything about it.

In addition, young mothers use television to escape their problems. The terrible woes of the people on the soap operas make their problems seem less important. This means that they don't need to solve their own problems.

Although it may seem as if television is really great for older people, I think even my grandma would have more fun if she had more interests rather than just watching quiz shows. I know she has blotted out the "real world" when she expects us to act like the Cosby kids when she comes to visit.

In conclusion, I believe that television really can become an addiction that allows people of all ages to avoid facing their own problems and lose themselves in the problems of other people.

ANALYSIS

This essay has a traditional structure; the first paragraph introduces the topic, and even suggests the chronological organization of the essay. Each of the next four paragraphs has a clear topic sentence and provides details that develop it. The concluding paragraph, although only one sentence in length, restates the main idea. The essay is, therefore, clearly unified around the writer's opinion, which the writer tries to prove in a logical fashion. The writer effectively employs transitional words to relate the main ideas, varied sentence structure, and controlled vocabulary. Although the writer misspells *pastime,* uses the colloquial word *kids,* and has some problem with parallelism, repetition, and pronoun usage, the essay is well written.

SAMPLE ESSAY: Satisfactory

I do not agree with the given statement. I think that instead of being bad for people, television not only does not blot out the real world but, instead, gives the person watching it a chance to experience the real world, even places he can't possibly go and may never get a chance to go.

For instance, I've learned a lot about the Vietnam War by watching TV. For a while, I heard things about it, about how some of the veterans didn't feel as if they were welcomed right when they came back from that war. I didn't understand what was the matter. Then they built a special memorial in Washington for the veterans that didn't come back. Since then, I have seen a lot of programs that showed what went on in Vietnam, and I've heard Vietnam vets talk about what happened to them. I think that that war has become very real to me because of TV.

Television educates us about the dangers of growing up in America today. I've seen good programs about the dangers of using drugs, about teenage pregnancy and what happens if you try to keep the baby, about eating too much cholesterol (That doesn't matter to me yet, but my dad needs to watch that!), and also anorexia. These are things we all need to know about, and TV has told about them so we know what to do.

I really am convinced that television brings the real world into your house. I think us kids today know a lot more about the real world than our grandparents did who grew up without television.

ANALYSIS

This essay is competently written. The writer takes one position and develops it. The first paragraph provides a clear introduction, and paragraphs two and three develop the thesis. Generalized examples are provided. The final paragraph concludes the essay. The essay contains some problems in correct usage, colloquial words like *kids,* and a lack of concrete examples. (What, specifically, did the writer learn about the Vietnam War?) Sentences lack variety in length and construction, with many beginning with the pronoun "I." Ideas are not always clearly related to each other. The theme contains unnecessary repetition and errors in pronoun use. All of these flaws combine to make the essay merely satisfactory.

SAMPLE ESSAY: Unsatisfactory

On the one hand, I think television is bad, But it also does some good things for all.of us. For instants, my little sister thought she wanted to be a policeman until she saw police shows on TV. Then she learned how dangerous it is and now she wants to be an astronaut. I guess she didn't watch the Challenger explode often enough to scare her out of that.

But the bad thing about' television programs are the ideas it puts in kids heads. Like violent things happen on television, and little kids see it and don't know that other people hurt when they are hit, battered up, beat, shot, ect. Then the kids go out and try to knock their friends around and think if they are strong and handsome that they can get their own way whatever happens. Even parents sometimes have trouble controling their own kids because of too much TV. Of course that's partly because the parents watch too much too when they .should of been taking care of the kids they necklooted them watching television.

So I think that television has both it's good and it's bad points. I'd hate to see us get rid of it all together, but I wonder if I'll let my kids watch it when I have them. It sometimes puts bad ideas in their heads.

ANALYSIS

The failure of the writer of this essay to take one opinion and clearly develop it weakens the essay. The writer does try to give specific examples, but the details in the introductory paragraph.would be more appropriate later in the essay. The apparent topic sentence of the second paragraph suggests a discussion of the results of children watching too much television, but the writer discusses the parents' viewing in the same paragraph. The last sentence of the conclusion repeats the idea of the topic sentence of the second paragraph. The writer does not express his/her ideas in precise fashion ("Even parents sometimes have trouble controling (sic) their own kids because of too much TV.") or provide clear relationships between them. The essay also contains colloquialisms and errors in pronoun use, spelling, use of the apostrophe, and sentence construction. Overall, this essay is not satisfactory.

4.8 Problem/Solution

Another common logical pattern for organization is that of *problem and solution*. In this pattern, the writer begins by stating a problem that needs to be solved, and continuing by explaining and describing the background and nature of the problem (perhaps its causes and negative effects), and possibly ends by offering a way or ways to remedy the probem.

The writer employs two patterns of organization for this type of paper. In the first pattern, the writer (1) states the problem in the introduction, (2) discusses the background and history, (3) reviews the relevant known complications of the problem and the major forms that it takes (social, political, etc.), and then (4) offers a solution.

In the second pattern, the writer follows the same sequence. In the opening of the paper, however, the writer not only states the problem, but offers a way or ways to solve it, rather than offering solutions in the conclusion. A writer frequently employs this pattern in scientific research or technical studies in scholarly disciplines and social and technical science courses. (For a fuller discussion of the format and sections of a research paper in the technical and social sciences, see Chapter 7.) For example, a course in sociology might require a student to write a paper on an important social question, e.g., "How can we prevent petty crime among urban teenagers?" Typically, the writer will do research to offer solutions for such a problem.

An English class may call for an essay in response to a significant problem brought up by a famous author for class discussion. The essay would also call for the student to offer personal solutions. The *thesis* would be a solution to a particular problem, and as in any other essay, it is necessary to supply evidence in support of the solution.

Problem Solving Example:

Q In the last 20 years, the deterioration of the environment has become a growing concern among both scientists and ordinary citizens. Choose one pressing environmental problem, explain its negative impact, and discuss possible solutions.

A Three sample essays follow, which represent possible responses to the essay topic. Compare your own response to those given on the next few pages. Allow the strengths and weaknesses of the sample essays to help you critique your own essay and improve your writing skills.

SAMPLE ESSAY: Well-written

There are many pressing environmental problems facing both this country and the world today. Pollution, the misuse and squandering of resources, and the cavalier attitude many people express all contribute to the problem. But one of the most pressing problems this country faces is the apathetic attitude many Americans have towards recycling.

Why is recycling so imperative? There are two major reasons. First, recycling previously used materials conserves precious national resources. Many people never stop to think that reserves of metal ores are not unlimited. There is only so much gold, silver, tin, and other metals in the ground. Once it has all been mined, there will never be any more unless we recycle what has already been used.

Second, the United States generates more solid waste daily than any other country on earth. Our disposable consumer culture consumes fast food meals in paper or styrofoam containers, uses disposable diapers with plastic liners that do not biodegrade, receives pounds, if not tons, of unsolicited junk mail every year, and relies more and more on prepackaged rather than fresh food.

No matter how it is accomplished, increased recycling is essential. We have to stop covering our land with garbage, and the best ways to do this are to reduce our dependence on prepackaged goods and to minimize the amount of solid waste disposed of in landfills. The best way to reduce solid waste is to recycle it. Americans need to band together to recycle, to preserve our irreplaceable natural resources, reduce pollution, and preserve our precious environment.

ANALYSIS

This essay presents a clearly defined thesis, and the writer elaborates on this thesis in a thoughtful and sophisticated manner. The writer presents and explores various aspects of the problem under consideration along with possible solutions to these problems. The support provided for the writer's argument is convincing and logical. There are few usage or mechanical errors to interfere with the writer's ability to communicate effectively. This writer demonstrates a comprehensive understanding of the rules of written English.

SAMPLE ESSAY: Satisfactory

A pressing environmental problem today is the way we are cutting down too many trees and not planting any replacements for them. Trees are beneficial in many ways, and without them, many environmental problems would be much worse.

One of the ways trees are beneficial is that, like all plants, they take in carbon dioxide and produce oxygen. They can actually help clean the air this way. When too many trees are cut down in a small area, the air in that area is not as good and can be unhealthy to breath.

Another way trees are beneficial is that they provide homes for many types of birds, insects, and animals. When all the trees in an area are cut down, these animals lose their homes and sometimes they can die out and become extinct that way. Like the spotted Owls in Oregon, that the loggers wanted to cut down the trees they lived in. If the loggers did cut down all the old timber stands that the spotted owls lived in, the owls would have become extinct.

But the loggers say that if they can't cut the trees down then they will be out of work, and that peoples' jobs are more important than birds. The loggers; can do two things—they can either get training so they can do other jobs, or they can do what they should have done all along, and start replanting trees. For every mature tree they cut down, they should have to plant at least one tree seedling.

Cutting down the trees that we need for life, and. that lots of other species depend on, is a big environmental problem that has a lot of long term consaquences, Trees are too important for all of us to cut them down without thinking about the future.

ANALYSIS

This essay has a clear thesis, which the author supports with good examples. But the writer shifts between the chosen topic, which is that indiscriminate tree-cutting is a pressing environmental problem, and a list of the ways in which trees are beneficial, and a discussion about the logging profession. Also, while there are few mistakes in usage and mechanics, the writer does have some problems with sentence structure. The writing is pedestrian and the writer does not elaborate on the topic as much as he or she could have. The writer fails to provide the kind of critical analysis that the topic required.

SAMPLE ESSAY: Unsatisfactory

The most pressing environmental problem today is that lots of people and companies don't care about the environment, and they do lots of things that hurt the environment.

People throw littur out car windows and don't use trash cans, even if their all over the park, soda cans and fast food wrappers are all over the place. Cigarette butts are the worst cause the filters never rot. Newspapers and junk mail get left to blow all over the neighborhood, and beer bottles too.

Companies pollute the air and the water. Sometimes the ground around a company has lots of tocsins in it. Now companies can buy credits from other companies that let them pollute the air even more. They dump all kinds of chemacals into lakes and river that kills off the fish and causes acid rain and kills off more fish and some trees and small animuls and insects and then noone can go swimming or fishing in the lake.

People need to respect the environment because we only have one planet, and if we keep polluting it pretty soon nothing will grow and then even the people will die.

ANALYSIS

The writer of this essay does not define his or her thesis for this essay. Because of this lack of a clear thesis, the reader is left to infer the topic from the body of the essay. It is possible to perceive the writer's intended thesis; however, the support for this thesis is very superficial. The writer presents a list of common complaints about polluters, without any critical discussion of the problems and possible solutions. Many sentences are run-ons and the writer has made several spelling errors. While the author manages to communicate his or her position on the issue, he or she does so on such a superficial level and with so many errors in usage and mechanics that he/she fails to demonstrate an ability to communicate effectively.

4.9   Comparison/Contrast

Comparison/contrast papers call upon the student to take two (or more) ideas, things, or people and show how they *contrast,* or *differ from,* one another; and how they *compare* or *are similar to one another.* The two fundamental patterns of comparison/contrast papers are block by block or point by point. In order to compare five different qualities about two different things, a writer could organize his/her paper into two big middle sections (after the introduction and before the conclusion), each of which compares and/or contrasts the same five qualities about all the things under discussion. For example to compare two different cars, a Mustang and a Corvette, the writer can organize the discussion so that the same five qualities for each car in the same order in each block are addressed: e.g., compare Mustangs and Corvettes with respect to (1) design, (2) power, (3) road ability, (4) resale value, and (5) cost. The writer would then write about each car, positives and negatives, section by section in the same pattern and in the same order:

Mustangs: quality 1, quality 2, quality 3, quality 4, quality 5; v.
Corvettes: quality 1, quality 2, quality 3, quality 4, quality 5.

The second possibility for organization in comparison/contrast papers is that of *point-by-point* comparisons. In this pattern, the writer obviously compares Mustangs and Corvettes point by point while the block-by-block pattern is inverted so that the organization looks like this:

Quality 1: Mustangs v. Corvettes

Quality 2: Mustangs v. Corvettes

Quality 3: Mustangs v. Corvettes

Quality 4: Mustangs v. Corvettes

Quality 5: Mustangs v. Corvettes

Often, professors request that students use comparison/contrast patterns of organization to compare or contrast the advantages and disadvantages of two or more ideas, things, or people. For an argumentative essay, maintain a thesis that demonstrates, by using the organizational pattern of comparison/contrast, the advantages and disadvantages, or the relative value between two or several ideas, things, or people. In the case of the Mustangs v. Corvettes comparison/contrast, use the five points to show that in each case, the Mustang is superior to the Corvette and is more advantageous to buy and own. Comparison/contrast patterns can also be used to merely explain or inform the reader of the similarities and differences between the two models.

Problem Solving Example:

Q In the selection from *Leviathan,* Thomas Hobbes distinguishes between Right of Nature and Law of Nature. Write an essay in which you explain Hobbes's distinction between the two. What is the relationship between them?

From Part 1, Chapter 14. Of the First and Second Natural Laws

The Right of Nature, which writers commonly call *jus naturale,* is the liberty each man hath to use his own power as he will himself for the preservation of his own nature, that is to say, of his own life; and consequently of doing anything which in his own judgment and reason he shall conceive to be the aptest means thereunto.

By Liberty is understood, according to the proper signification of the word, the absence of external impediments, which impediments may oft take away part of a man's power to do what he would, but cannot hinder him from using the power left him according as his judgment and reason shall dictate to him.

A Law of Nature *(lex naturalis)* is a precept or general rule found out by reason, by which a man is forbidden to do that which is destructive of his life or taketh away the means of preserving the same; and to omit that by which he thinketh it may be best preserved. For though they that speak of this subject use to confound *Jus* and *Lex, Right* and *Law;* yet they ought to be distinguished, because Right consisteth in liberty to do or to forbear, whereas Law determineth and bindeth to one of them: so that Law and Right differ as much as obligation and liberty, which is one and the same matter are inconsistent.

And because the condition of man (as hath been declared in the precedent chapter) is a condition of war of every one against every one, in which case every one is governed by his own reason, and there is nothing he can make use of that may not be a help unto him in preserving his life against his enemies: it followeth that in such a condition every man has a right to every thing even to one another's body. And therefore as long as this natural right of every man to every thing endureth, there can be no security to any man (how strong or wise soever he be) of living out the time which nature ordinarily alloweth men to live. And consequently it is a precept, or general rule of reason, *That every man ought to endeavor peace as far as he has hope of obtaining it; and when he cannot obtain it, that he may seek and use all helps and advantages of war.* The first branch of which rule containeth the first and fundamental law of nature, which is to seek peace and follow it. The second, the sum of the right of nature, which is, *by all means we can to defend ourselves.*

From this fundamental law of nature, by which men are commanded to endeavor peace, is derived this second law: *That a man be willing, when others are so too, as far-forth as for peace and defence of himself he shall think necessary, to lay down this right to all things, and be contented with so much liberty against other men as he would allow other men against himself.* For as long as any man holdeth this right of doing anything he liketh, so long are all men in the condition of war. But if other men will not lay down their right, as well as he, then there is no reason for anyone to divest himself of his. For that were to expose himself to prey (which no man is bound to) rather than to dispose himself to peace. This is the law of the Gospel: *Whatsoever you require that others should do to you, that do ye to them.*

 This Answer provides three sample essays that represent possible responses to the essay topic. Compare your own response to those given on the next few pages. Allow the strengths and weaknesses of the sample essays to help you critique your own essay and improve your writing skills.

SAMPLE ESSAY: Well-written

Hobbes distinguishes between the Right of Nature, which basically looks only to self-interest, and the Law of Nature, which looks to the common good. But because self-interest ultimately depends on the common good, the Law of Nature must take priority over the Right of Nature.

By "Right of Nature," Hobbes means the liberty to preserve one's life through any means the individual's reason deems necessary. Under the Right of Nature, no external force may restrain man from taking any action he pleases to defend or preserve himself.

In contrast, a Law of Nature is based not on Liberty, but obligation, and forbids man to do things that would destroy his life or destroy the means of preserving his life. Both Right and Law derive from reason, but the former derives from an individual's reason whereas the latter derives from a broader perspective.

To fully understand the relationship between the two, it is necessary to understand Hobbes' conception of the human condition. Because he believes man's natural condition is a state of war, it follows that the Right of Nature would entitle men to destroy one another, in which case individual and group security are impossible. Hence a broader perspective is needed to create security. That broader perspective suggests that all men should pursue peace, which is Hobbes' first Law of Nature. Only when peace cannot be achieved may the Right of Nature—to protect oneself—be exercised. Furthermore, Hobbes derives a second Law of Nature from the first; in order to preserve peace and protect himself, man must be willing to give up unrestrained liberty if he wishes others to give up unrestrained liberty in their actions toward him. What Hobbes argues for, then, is a social contract which recognizes not only the desirability but the necessity of subordinating individual self-interest to the group interest even from the narrow perspective of self-preservation. In a constant state of war in which each individual does as he pleases, no individual will prosper. Hence the Right of Nature cannot take priority over the Law of Nature if chaos is to be avoided.

ANALYSIS

This question asks the student to do more than explain the distinction between two concepts as expressed in a fairly difficult essay. The student must understand the selection from Hobbes's *Leviathan* in order to write a good essay, but must do more than simply summarize what Hobbes says. There are several stages in Hobbes's explanation, and the student must demonstrate understanding of those stages. Moreover, the two concepts spring from certain assumptions and depend on other background ideas that must be explained or clarified. Finally, the relationship between the two concepts is more subtle than first appears, and the student must make sure that he/she clarifies that relationship.

In the sample essay, the writer provides a brief explanation of the essential difference between Law of Nature and Right of Nature and states the ultimate relationship between the two in the first paragraph. The second paragraph then explains, in clear, contemporary English and in more detail, what Hobbes means by Right of Nature. The third paragraph explains what Hobbes means by Law of Nature, contrasting the source of the Law of Nature with the source of the Right of Nature. The relationship between the two, briefly stated in the writer's first paragraph (that the Law of Nature must take priority over the Right of Nature because self-interest ultimately depends on the common good), is complex, involving several steps; hence the writer appropriately spends more time on this aspect of the question than on any other part of the essay. The writer explains that the relationship between the two depends on an understanding of a prior concept (Hobbes's conception of the human condition) and on several conclusions that follow from that concept. Finally, the writer restates the central argument of the excerpt in language that Hobbes might not recognize but that makes Hobbes's chief position clear. Only by tracing the several stages of Hobbes's argument can the student arrive at an adequate explanation of the two concepts that the question asks the student to analyze.

SAMPLE ESSAY: Satisfactory

Hobbes makes a distinction between the Right of Nature and the Law of Nature. He believes the Right of Nature looks to self-interest while the Law of Nature looks to the common good. Therefore, the Right of Nature must come before the Law of Nature.

The Right of Nature is the freedom to preserve one's life bye any means the individual thinks is necessary. Under the Right of Nature, no external force may prevent man from taking any action he desires to defend or preserve himself.

In contrast, the Law of Nature is based on obligation. The law forbids man from doing anything that would destroy his life or the means of preserving it. Both concepts come from reason. However, Right of Nature comes from individual reason while the Law of Nature comes from a broader perspective.

To see the relationship between the two, one must understand Hobbes's conception of the human condition. He seas man's natural condition as being in a constant state of war, so the Right of Nature gives man the power to destroy one another, making individual and group security impossible. A broader perspective is needed to create security. This is Hobbes's first Law of Nature that suggests all men should pursue peace. When peace cannot be achieved, the Right of Nature is exercised. Hobbes derives a second Law of Nature from the first in order to preserve peace and protect himself. Hobbes advocates a social contract which places group interest before self-interest and self-preservation. In a constant state of war, man will act as he pleases and no individual will prosper; therefore, the the Right of Nature cannot take precedent over the Law of Nature.

ANALYSIS

A comparison/contrast essay explains the similarities or differences between two concepts. The introduction of a comparison essay names the two concepts that will be compared or contrasted and tells the reader how the concepts are alike or different. The body of a comparison essay can be developed in many different ways. For example, the writer can explain the first concept thoroughly and then go on to explain the second concept. Another method the writer can employ is to give parallel information about the second concept as the first is explained. It is also possible for the writer to discuss one element being compared or contrasted as it relates to each concept. The writer must use a transitional phrase, such as "in contrast" or "on the other hand" to let the reader know the second concept is being discussed. The writer of this essay has selected the first method.

The introduction tells the reader that this essay will discuss the difference between Hobbes's Right of Nature and his Law of Nature. The basis of the contrast will be self-interest (Right of Nature) versus common good (Law of Nature). Paragraph two defines the Right of Nature as the freedom to preserve one's life. The paragraph contains one word choice error: "Bye" should be "by." Paragraph three begins with the phrase, "In contrast," to show the reader that the second concept will be discussed. The essay writer explains that the Law of Nature prevents man from self-destruction The writer also explains the relationship between the Law of Nature and the Right of Nature, saying they both come from reason. Paragraph four explains Hobbes's concept of the human condition, which states that man is constantly at war. The writer feels that in war man will do as he pleases and the Law of Nature will prevail. The paragraph contains one word choice error: "Seas" should be "sees."

This essay compares two difficult concepts, so it is important that they both be explained with appropriate language and clear organization. For the most part, the writer does a good job, but the essay does have several weaknesses that distract from its strength. It might have been preferable, for instance, to have developed each of the earliest paragraphs in the essay in order to begin by giving the reader a clear understanding of the elements being contrasted, and in order to give the essay better balance. The word choice errors take away from the essay writer's contrast of the Law of Nature and the Right of Nature. These errors, and the fact that the writer does not fully develop each idea, make the otherwise well-written essay imperfect.

SAMPLE ESSAY: Unsatisfactory

Hobbes said that there was a difference between the Right of Nature and the Law of Nature. He believed the Right of Nature looks to self-interest while the Law of nature looks to the common good. Since self-interest depends on the common good. The Law of Nature is more important than the Right of Nature.

The Right of Nature is being free to preserve one's life by any means necessary. In addition, no outside force may prevent man from taking any action he pleases to defend or preserve himself.

In contrast, the Law of Nature is based on obligation. The law forbids man from doing anything that would destroy his life or destroy the means of preserving it.

To see the relationship between the two. An individual must understand Hobbes' conception of the human condition as being in a constant state of war. The Right of Nature entitles man to destroy one another. This makes individual and group security impossible. A broader perspective is needed to create security: That is the Law of Nature which says men should pursue peace. When there is no peace. The Right of

Nature—to protect oneself—is exercised. Hobbes creates a second Law of Nature, so man can preserve peace and protect himself.

ANALYSIS

This essay is somewhat short and choppy, and none of the ideas are fully developed or clearly explained. In a comparison/contrast essay, it is important first to extensively explain each element that is being compared. This essay does not establish the basis of the argument before launching into the comparison/contrast.

The introduction states that the Right of Nature and the Law of Nature will be contrasted. It does not, however, establish how or why they will be contrasted, or give the reader any sense of the importance of the concepts, or any desire to read the remainder of the essay. It does not effectively establish a background for the argument to follow. The paragraph contains one error, a sentence fragment ("Since self-interest depends on the common good").

The next paragraph explains the Right of Nature. The third paragraph begins with "In contrast." This tells the reader that the second concept (Law of Nature) will be discussed. Both concepts—Right of Nature and Law of Nature—are quite complicated. The brief definitions in these paragraphs do not sufficiently enlighten the reader and are not convincing in displaying the writer's knowledge of the subject.

The final paragraph explores further how one must understand Hobbes's conception of the human condition as it relates to the Law of Nature and the Right of Nature. This paragraph, though it contains two fragments ("To see the relationship between the two" and "When there is no peace"), functions effectively as a conclusion to the essay, and is perhaps the only place where the ideas are fully developed.

This essay follows the comparison/contrast format very well. It does not, however, take the time to develop each element within this framework. Furthermore, it has several sentence fragments, which detract from the strength of the essay. This essay requires a lot of revision and expansion in order to become a satisfactory essay.

4.10 Argumentation

Argumentation seeks to persuade the reader that something is true, real, or probable. It is the most complex form of organization in essay writing, and usually requires all the skills involved in using the other patterns. All of the patterns of organization explained above may be used to convince a reader of the truth, reality, or probability of a thesis.

Recall from Chapter 2 the discussion of the *thesis* or the main point. Once the thesis is determined move to a discussion which proves the point, using the organizational pattern that best supports the logic of the position. In order to make a case for the idea that Mustangs are better than Corvettes, put to use the best evidence there is to support the five points, as in the example 4.9. Comparison/contrast could be the best pattern to use. In some cases, however, a combination of patterns might better prove the thesis.

Many years ago Aristotle, the ancient Greek philosopher, stated that there are three fundamental kinds of arguments: *ethical, pathetic,* and *logical.* To this day, these three types govern the formation of arguments.

In the *ethical argument,* the writer *persuades the reader by virtue of his or her character.* If for example, today, Abraham Lincoln were to argue for the freedom of the slaves, the chances are that he would be believed—not primarily because of the justice of his case, but because his reputation precedes him. In this type of argument, the audience trusts the person arguing a great deal, and they tend to believe whatever the person says. A recognized expert in a given field could also offer an ethical argument. For instance, a nationally recognized environmental scientist might argue for the preservation of the whales as a species, and above and beyond the facts and statistics he or she might offer, the fact that he or she is a trusted authority on the subject would tend to persuade the audience to accept the scientist's point of view. This sort of argumentation is also the key to propaganda, a topic to be addressed later.

In *pathetic argumentation,* the writer persuades the audience to believe him or her not by the power of the writer's reputation or personality, but by the emotions that move them to believe the writer. A writer may appeal to the righteousness of his or her thesis by appealing to the reader's emotions about the issues. The writer could contend, for example, that dogs should not be kept in the basement because being in a basement makes them very sad and "just think of your own pet dog in the basement—isn't that a cruel thing to do?" The reader tends to be moved to agree with the writer not because of the facts of the situation but because of the sympathy the reader has for the person or situation. In this case, the writer is not *reasoning with the audience, but rather is attempting to sway the audience to a position by persuading them to sympathize or empathize with the thesis.*

This sort of argumentation, while it can be used for good purposes, is often an underhanded and scurrilous way to persuade people to do things against their better judgment. More often than not, propagandists use *pathetic argument* to have people believe in or act upon an issue despite the power of their own reason.

The final form of argumentation, *logical argumentation,* stems from the Greek word for "order," "reason," or "the word." In this form of argument, the writer appeals to the audience's sense of reason and logic to persuade the audience to a particular point of view. The best writers will use the powers of all three forms of argument to convince their readers of the truth, probability, or reality of their position. Professors require students to understand the qualities of *ethical* and *pathetic* argumentation, but they usually emphasize *logical argumentation.*

Central to the control of a good argument is the command of logic and the presentation of evidence. The arrangement of ideas is also extremely important. The *rhetoric,* or presentation of ideas, is almost as important as the logic or reasonableness of ideas. Consequently, take into account the power of the rhetoric, or *delivery of the argument.* As in the case of personal argument, a logical argument requires the writer to be careful about how he or she presents an unpopular or controversial idea.

There is no need to argue or convince those people who are already in accordance with the idea. *The purpose of a good argument is to*

convince those who are most likely to disagree with you. The presentation of a good logical argument might look like this:

THE RHETORICAL SHAPE OF ARGUMENTATION

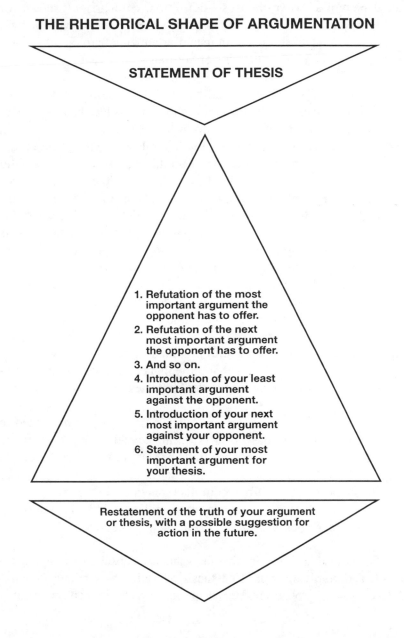

STATEMENT OF THESIS

1. Refutation of the most important argument the opponent has to offer.
2. Refutation of the next most important argument the opponent has to offer.
3. And so on.
4. Introduction of your least important argument against the opponent.
5. Introduction of your next most important argument against your opponent.
6. Statement of your most important argument for your thesis.

Restatement of the truth of your argument or thesis, with a possible suggestion for action in the future.

A writer may develop an argument using any of the organizational patterns in order to support the logic of the thesis. Whatever organizational pattern a writer chooses—definition, comparison/contrast, or problem/solution—the best way to dispute the opponent's viewpoint is to dismiss the opposition's anticipated arguments with counter arguments, as the writer develops his or her thesis.

Most students' arguments fail because they argue only their own side. For instance, a student might argue that cats are the best pets to own because they are small, take up little space, don't eat very much, and can take care of themselves for several days without attention. However, an opponent to that thesis might grant that these are valid reasons for why cats are good pets, but then raise the issues that cats cannot protect people the way dogs can, that cats often destroy furniture and rugs with their claws, and that cats rarely show loyalty to the owner. Consequently, the argument that fails to address these ideas is inadequate. An argument that refutes dog lovers would have to address the strong arguments of those who claim that dogs are better pets than cats in order to be effective. To argue only for the merits of cats is not a rational, or *logical* position because it does not include, account for, or overrule the logically relevant arguments of the opponent.

In any prosecution of a useful argument, a good writer will avoid any logical errors or fallacies that the opponent might summon to defeat him or her (for a review of logical fallacies see Chapter 2.6.2).

Any good argument is only as good as the evidence presented to support the position of the writer. After the key terms of the argument are defined, a variety of evidence must be stated to support the thesis. Most instructors will request that at least three kinds of evidence be used to support a thesis. To accomplish this goal, a student could use (1) facts and statistics, (2) anecdotal examples, and (3) the testimony of authorities to support his/her argumentative position.

The writer must be sure that facts and statistics are current and not slighted arbitrarily in favor of the thesis, as well as be sure that the anecdotal evidence is probable and that it appeals to the reader's common sense.

Also, be sure that the authorities used are truly experts in their field, e.g., Lamarck should not be used as an authority on evolution because he has been long outdated and overridden by Darwin.

Problem Solving Example:

Q Many leaders have suggested over the last few years that instead of a military draft we should require all young people to serve the public in some way for a period of time. The service could be military or any other reasonable form of public service. Do you agree or disagree with such sentiments? Support your opinion with specific examples from history, current events, literature, or personal experience.

A This Answer provides three sample essays which represent possible responses to the essay topic. Compare your own response to those given on the next few pages. Allow the strengths and weaknesses of the sample essays to help you critique your own essay and improve your writing skills.

SAMPLE ESSAY: Well-written

The cynic in me wants to react to the idea of universal public service for the young with a reminder about previous complaints aimed at the military draft. These complaints suggest that wars might never be fought if the first people drafted were the adult leaders and lawmakers. Still the idea of universal public-service sounds good to this concerned citizen who sees everywhere—not just in youth—the effects of a selfish and self indulgent culture.

One reads and hears constantly about young people who do not care about the problems of our society. These youngsters seem interested in money and the luxuries money can buy. They do not want to work from the minimum wage up, but want instead to land a high paying job without "paying their dues." An informal television news survey of high school students a few years ago suggested that students had the well entrenched fantasy that with no skills or higher education they would not accept a job paying less than $20 an hour. Perhaps universal service helping out in an urban soup kitchen for six months would instill a sense of selflessness rather than selfishness.

The shiny gleam of a new expensive sports sedan bought on credit by a recent accounting student reflects self indulgence that might be toned down by universal service. That self indulgence may reflect merely a lack of discipline, but it also may reflect a lack of purpose in life. Philosophers, theologians, and leaders of all types suggest throughout the ages that money and objects do not ultimately satisfy. Helping others—service to our fellow human beings—often does. Universal public service for that accounting student might require a year helping low income or senior citizens prepare income tax forms. This type of service would lessen the drive for self indulgence, give the person some experience in the real world, and also demonstrate that it is possible to find satisfaction that is not dependant on material things.

Universal service might also help young people restore their faith in their nation and what it means to them. Yes, this is the land of opportunity, but it is also a land of forgotten people, and it is a land that faces outside threats. Part of the requisite public service should remind young people of their past and of their responsibility to the future.

ANALYSIS

This essay uses a traditional structure: the first paragraph states the topic, the second and third present development with specific examples from personal observation, and the fourth ends the essay, but is not as strong a conclusion as it could be. The writer probably ran out of time. The essay as a whole is unified and uses pertinent examples to support the opinion stated. The sentence structure is well varied, and the vocabulary is effective.

SAMPLE ESSAY: Satisfactory

In the U.S. today, when a boy turns 18 he is obligated by law, to register for the military draft. This is done so that in case of a war or something catastrophic these boys and men can be called on for active duty in the military. It is good to know that we will have the manpower in case of a war but my opinion on the military draft is negative, I don't like the idea of forcing someone to sign up at a certain age for something that they don't want to happen, Of course, I know that we need some sort of military manpower on hand just in case, but it would be so much better if it was left to the individual to decide what area to serve in and what time.

When a boy turns 18, he's a rebel of sorts, He doesn't want someone telling him what to do and when to do it; he's just beginning to live. In Switzerland, when a boy turns 18, he goes into some branch of the military for a time of training, He is given his gun, uniform and badge number, Then, once a year for about two weeks he suits up for retraining, He does this until he is about 65 years old. Now in a way this is like a draft but the men love it and feel that it is honorable. I thing that they like it because it does not discriminate and their jobs pay them for the time away. Switzerland seems to give the 18 year old somewhat of a choice what division to go in and whether or not to join, They're not as strict on joining as we are so it's more of an honorable thing to do.

Of course, I'd love to see it as strictly up to the individual but it can't be that way. We have too many enemies that we might go to war with and we would need a strong military. Switzerland has nothing to worry about as long as they have their banks.

ANALYSIS
This essay displays competence in overall thought. It does not state its topic quite as well as Essay I. The extended example of Swiss military conscription is the main strength of the essay. The writer hedges a bit but manages to convey an opinion. Sentences have some variety, and the vocabulary is competent. Some spelling and grammatical errors interfere with the effectiveness of the communication.

SAMPLE ESSAY: Unsatisfactory
I agree with the many leaders who suggest we require young people to serve the public in some way, rather than the military draft.

There are several reasons this could benefit our country. The first being giving the young people, perhaps just out of high school, with no job experience, an opportunity to give something to his community. In return for this, he gains self respect and pride.

Whether it be taking flowers to shut-ins or just stopping for a chat in a rest home, a young person would have gained something and certainly given, perhaps hope, to that elder person. I can tell from my own experience, not quite old enough for the military draft, how enriched I feel when visiting the elderly. They find joy in the simplest things, which in turn, teaches me I should do the same.

Another thing gained by doing voluntary type work, is a sense of caring about doing the job right—quality! If you can't do it for your country, what else matters?

ANALYSIS

This essay has major faults, not the least of which is the lack of a clear sense of overall organization. The thoughts do have some coherence, but they don't seem to fit into a plan, except to express agreement with the statement. Examples from personal observation do help, but the paragraphs are not well developed. Several severe grammatical problems interfere with the communication.

CHAPTER 5

Writing About Literature

5.1 Elements of the Work

When writing about literature, the professor requires that the student analyzes elements of the work in order to show an understanding of that work.

Usually the professor requires that the student understands the time in which a piece of literature was written, not the time in which it is set. To that end, a professor may ask that some historical analysis be included in an essay. For example, a student would probably want to include the fact that George Orwell wrote *1984* in 1948, while, as the title indicates, the novel itself is set in the then future of 1984.

Genres, or *literary forms,* continue to be the most standard approach to the study of literature at the undergraduate level. The organization of an essay about literature will still be that of introduction, body or middle development, and conclusion, but the elements under study will change somewhat from genre to genre. For example, the elements under study in the analysis of a work of *fiction* will include: *plot, character (and characterization), dialogue, setting, symbolic language, style,* and *theme.* In *drama,* these elements are very much the same, with the exception of studying not just the structural elements of the play, but also *the elements of production or staging,* which will include the *quality of the set, type of stage (in-the-round or dividing curtain), lighting, choreography, timing or pace,* and the *quality or style of the acting.*

In *poetry,* however, the elements shift again to a focus of *language* and *intensive elements.* The student also examines how the writer uses these elements of *figurative language* and *rhyme and meter* to move the reader to an aesthetic, ethical, or political response—including tears, laughter, and the whole range of emotions of which people are capable. The elements that are key to the *analysis of poetry* include *the narrator and* **persona** *(his or her voice), setting, rhyme (if any), metrical or rhythmic scheme, figurative language (including images, metaphors, and symbols), and mythical content (if any).* The job of the student who analyzes or interprets a poem is to show how these elements work together to produce the response that the student feels is the correct one to the poem.

Of course, in the case of the poem, a wide range of interpretation is possible for any given poem. While the student cannot prove that a poem means one thing rather than another, by demonstrating how a majority of the elements of its structure (rhyme scheme, figurative language, setting, and persona) work in concert to produce the same response, the student can *make a case that is probable* that his or her response to the poem is consistent with the language in the poem itself.

The student must be careful not to go on instinct alone, but have some proof backing up his or her ideas; analyzing poetry is not merely a matter of personal interpretation. While it is true that the understanding of a poem is a matter of interpretation, it is not a very useful one if the understanding of a poem is the result of some wild, personal impression alone. A strong interpretation of a poem, or any form of literature for that matter, would be an *informed* interpretation *based upon a careful critical reading and analysis of the structural elements which the author has used to create a certain effect or produce a given response in the reader.*

While everyone has a right to his or her opinion, that doesn't make an analysis of a poem true, real, or probable. For example, the opinion may be held that the world is flat, but there is a great deal of documented evidence to show that such an opinion is empty of truth. Professors will probably also speak about avoiding two other fallacies in criticizing, or analyzing literature: *the intentional fallacy* and *the pathetic fallacy.*

Critics consider the *intentional fallacy* a major error in analyzing literature. Simply put, the fallacy is in *reasoning about the purpose or theme of a work based on what is the author's own expressed intent, or what you believe to be the author's intent.* Critics reason, not from intent, but from the effects that the particular combination of structural elements in the work of literature seem to consistently produce in the readers. This has its pitfalls, too, but it is less vulnerable to sentimental or arbitrary interpretations than the critical argument for the meaning of a work based upon the author's supposed or expressed intent.

The *pathetic fallacy* is often discussed among critics in reference to Romantic literature, and is one in which the author holds that his or her feelings about nature are those of Nature itself. Much of Romantic poetry in English engages in this fallacy and leads to the *anthropomorphic* interpretation of nature and art. It is the notion that because someone is feeling something (for instance, pathos) in the presence of nature, it must be true of Nature itself.

Apart from a *plot summary,* a student may write several types of papers. These include a *character analysis,* a *study of the figurative language,* an *analysis of the use of narration or persona,* a *thematic analysis,* or a *structural analysis.* In each case, it is advisable to use the organizational patterns explained earlier to demonstrate your thesis (define or describe a character; compare and contrast metaphors or themes; or classify or categorize two or more works read in class).

5.2 The Structural Elements of Fiction, Drama, and Poetry

Just as a carpenter uses his chief tools to build the house he wants, so writers use the "tools" of their trade to "build" their drama, fiction, or poem to reach their audiences with an idea, feeling, or combination of ideas and feelings. In the section that follows, the *structural elements* of literature will be examined for what they are: the tools of the writer's trade, craft, or art. The student's job is to become critical of a work of literature, not based upon the sentiment of liking or not liking a work, but based on an *analysis of the use of the structural elements,* or some dominating combination of the structural elements, of any work so as to suggest the nature of or success of the presentation of its theme, idea, or overall effect.

A persistent device used in literature is that of *irony. Irony is a technique of indicating an intention or attitude opposite to that which is actually stated.* Authors depend upon irony for certain kinds of effects that make readers think or reflect on how unpredictable life can be.

Irony can take many forms. Perhaps the most common form is that of *dramatic irony.* In this form, the plot of a play or fiction may take a sudden unexpected turn that the audience was not prepared for earlier in the drama. For example, in Dickens's *Great Expectations,* Pip, the protagonist, believes that the scheming Miss Havisham is his benefactor. He treats her with respect and deference all his young life only to discover later in life that she had not been his benefactor at all. Instead, she had attempted to ruin his life by making him fall hopelessly in love with her protege, Estella. Pip learns later through his lawyer that his benefactor was a lowly, anonymous criminal whom Pip had fed and helped to hide. The *irony* lies in the *unexpected turn of events* that led to Pip's finding out that he had been—along with the reader—laboring under the illusion that Miss Havisham was his benefactor and guardian.

Other elements of literature can be ironic: characters who appear as villains who turn out to be heroes, and vice-versa; and poems that appear to be about one kind of theme, and end up ridiculing the theme or showing its opposite (read, for example, W.H. Auden's poem "The Unknown Citizen"). One of the common forms of dramatic irony is that *of poetic justice.*

Poetic justice occurs when a character, usually evil, ends up getting what he or she wanted done to others—a kind of inverse of the golden rule: *"to have done unto oneself or the evil character what the evil character had hoped would be done unto his antagonist."* Thus, in the case of Miss Havisham, who hoped to have Pip, like all men, destroyed by love the way she had been (left on her wedding day by her prospective husband), she is destroyed by her own hatred, and she burns horribly in a fire that Pip tries in vain to save her from. Estella, raised by Miss Havisham to destroy men, and Pip in particular, with her charms, finds herself married to a fool and a bore, imprisoned forever in a loveless life of duty and boredom.

Irony can also be linguistic. In this case the writer uses particular images, metaphors, or symbols to demonstrate the opposite of that for which they seem to be symbols. For instance a writer could have a narrator attribute particular qualities to one character, then depict that character engaged in actions that are contrary to the original assessment, thus changing the reader's perception of that character.

5.2.1 Point of View and the Narrator: Omniscient, Limited-Omniscient, Limited

In any fiction, there is always a *narrator,* or *someone or something who is telling the story to the reader.* Unlike the point of view that may be used in an essay (first person or third person, see Chapter 4), which is just the way the author chooses to talk about a given topic, the *point of view* in fiction greatly influences the understanding of the story by the reader. A writer may choose to use the *omniscient narrator* and use the third person form to tell the story as if the narrator were Godlike, or omniscient: all-seeing, all-knowing, able to be everywhere at once. This omniscient narrator seems to see everything that happens, and often talks to the reader from the page as though he or she were speaking from inside all the characters' heads, thinking their thoughts even as they think them themselves.

Through the words of the omniscient narrator, the reader sees all of the characters' thoughts. This is impossible in life and is merely advice to help the story move along effectively. The narrator thus functions as a unifying principle, keeping the story coherent and interesting. In one of the most famous uses of a narrator, Gustave Flaubert, the French novelist, uses his all-seeing powers as a kind of linguistic "trick" to enable the reader to see into the title character's, or, Madame Bovary's, own thoughts.

Thus, although it is actually the writer Gustave Flaubert who is making Madame Bovary have these thoughts, it seems as though the reader is hearing Madame Bovary's thoughts as she thinks them. This special twist on the insight of the omniscient narrator is another literary device called *the internal monologue.* This device enables readers to hear or read, through the power of the omniscient narrator, the internal thoughts of the character in question. This is an illusion, but it is another useful device for moving a story forward.

The *limited-omniscient* narrator is one who tells the story from the vantage point of the first person ("I first met Strether Martin in the streets of Paris in 1832...") and who usually already knows the outcome. With the *limited-omniscient narrator,* readers know all of the narrator's thoughts, but not other characters' thoughts, at which the narrator sometimes guesses. The limited-omniscient narrator thus becomes a character in the story itself. He or she will often display prejudices and opinions about the conflict and other characters in the story that are contrary to or other than those displayed by the other characters about whom the narrator reports.

The *limited* or *restricted* narrator is one who tells the story, not only with limited insight into what will happen next, but from his or her own position of prejudice, opinion, or conviction. Thus, in Herman Melville's famous *Bartleby the Scrivener,* the story of Bartleby unfolds through the eyes of a narrator who becomes a major character in the story. In most cases, the limited narrator is a major character in the story and helps to move the plot forward.

In poetry, the author assumes a special form of the narrator called a *persona*. The *persona* is the one who becomes a character and tells the poem. The persona may be a god, sometimes an animal, sometimes a character from history. The reader should not confuse the narrator of a poem with the writer of the poem. The poet, then, may often "tell" the poem in the voice of the imagined narrator, be it an animal, a god, or even an idea, and any understanding of the poem must take into account the nature of the *persona* of the narrator. In Robert Browning's "My Last Duchess," the comments the *persona* makes are as important as the painting about which the Duke speaks. This particular way of using a narrator/persona is called a *dramatic monologue* and uses a "speaker" as a particular character to "tell" the poem. T.S. Eliot's *The Love Song of J. Alfred Prufrock* is also a dramatic monologue.

5.2.2 Plot

The *plot* is the *storyline of the work in which one action after another occurs until the completion, end, or resolution of the conflict among the characters.* The elements in the plot include (1) *the introduction of the characters and opening of the action,* (2) *the complications of the action and the introduction of conflict,* (3) *the climax,* and (4) *the denouement or resolution of the conflict.*

At first, most students of English believe that to analyze a piece of fiction is merely to tell the story over again, or write what is called a *plot summary.* This doesn't serve much purpose except as a way to recap key events in the story. Sometimes, however, a professor may ask for a plot summary to see if material was read effectively.

Plot development begins with the introduction of a set of characters who embark upon a course of action that leads to some conflict between or among them. Most often, an author will present fiction or drama as a "second" universe. That is, it looks like the real world and universe, and it is peopled with characters who look and act like real people, but it is, of course, not the real universe in which actual people live but a fictional representation of it. This phenomenon is often called *"slice of life."* Put simply, it means that each story read or drama watched is a "slice" taken out of the "pie" of real life. Because the writer has chosen to write about this particular time rather than some other, the reader can experience this "slice" as if present in it. This phenomenon of presenting in a story or drama a "look" at a universe that appears just like the real one is called *verisimilitude,* and most novels, television sitcoms, and police melodramas use this technique. Thus is born the phrase that literature is often an "imitation of life." This makes the drama being watched, or the fiction being read, much easier to follow and believe.

Samuel Taylor Coleridge, a famous Romantic English writer and poet, once pointed out that in order to take part in a piece of literature, the reader or watcher must *"suspend [his or her] disbelief"* because he or she is watching or reading about a substitute universe. The reader must act as if he or she is actually watching a real universe—that the stage isn't a room with an exposed fourth wall through which he or she views the action, but is actually a room. In other words, the reader has to pretend. Without this ability, a reader cannot watch or read a piece of fiction or a drama with any degree of comfort or acceptance. The illusion of a second, virtual universe—just like the real one—is what makes the enjoyment of literature possible at all. Readers and viewers must immerse themselves in this illusion in order to enjoy it.

Once having brought into play a series of characters involved in a situation, the writer then introduces or develops a major conflict. This conflict—sometimes love, sometimes war, sometimes the lust for gold and riches, among other possibilities—develops until it reaches a *climax,* or the moment when the conflict reaches its peak or the tables turn forever in favor of the protagonist or the antagonist. One of the most common forms of *plot development* is that (1) boy meets girl, (2) boy gets girl, (3) boy loses girl, and (4) boy gets girl again. *Resolution* comes when all the strands of the plot reach a solution: for example, the two lovers live "happily ever after" or the police get the criminals. Writers do not always resolve storylines, however, and some—as in the famous case of *Huckleberry Finn,* by Mark Twain—are left for the reader to determine. In that novel, the title character tells the reader that he's going to "light out for the territory," and since he is only a boy, the reader must guess what will become of him and his life.

5.2.3 Paradigmatic v. Episodic

Plots in drama and fiction, while having the basic elements explained above, can be of two basic types: *episodic* or *paradigmatic.* The *episodic plot* is that in which one episode or event seems to happen after another in the logical progression of time, but without any other apparent logic. *Huckleberry Finn* is an excellent example of that. As Huck goes down the Mississippi with the escaped slave Jim, crazy things occur in rapid succession: they meet Huck's father; they meet two Shakespearean actors; they meet the Colonel, and so on. This is a plot often associated with the *picaresque novel,* so called because it is about the adventures of a young man or woman, usually an orphan, or *picaro,* who by virtue of his or her wits, manages to overcome the many obstacles thrown in his or her path, as in the case of Huck and Jim, who overcome all to keep their freedom.

A *paradigmatic plot,* however, is one in which one thing happens after another as though designed by fate or "the gods" (as in Sophocles' *Oedipus Rex),* or by a logic so compelling as to leave no doubt as to the links among the characters and the action (as in a mystery). *Paradigmatic plots* (so-called because they are built on a model puzzle, or *paradigm,* of logical sequence of cause and effect) are those most often associated with mysteries and detective melodramas, or the "whodunits" of the movies.

5.2.4 Suspense, Flashback, and Foreshadowing

Writers use these common plot devices to create excitement and raise expectations in their audiences.

Writers generate *suspense* when they create an expectation in the plot between two or more of the characters in conflict, or between characters and impending events. The reader *expects something dan-*

gerous or critical to happen at any moment, or in the very next "moment" of the drama or storyline. Sometimes, the event will happen as expected and sometimes it won't, with the writer giving false signals and expectations, hoping to surprise the reader.

One of the devices used to create suspense is that of *foreshadowing,* in which the author uses some prop, a bit of dialogue, or a reference to some imagery or symbol that suggests to the reader a possibility or mode of future action. Chekov, for example, the famous Russian playwright, said that if a pistol is over the fireplace in the first act, it should be used by the last act, or it shouldn't be in the play at all. One of Chekov's characters might say in the first act to his rival, "You know, Markov, somebody could get killed with that pistol." By Act III, Markov and the speaker are in a duel and one gets killed with the pistol. A continual reference to some upcoming event, either through props, dialogue, or imagery, will build suspense and create an expectation within the reader, sometimes even without the readers themselves knowing why they are feeling anxious, expectant, or concerned.

Flashback is a plot device in which the narrator of a fiction, drama, or movie (as a voiceover, or a voice offstage) speaks in the present and relates a tale that happened in the recent or distant past. Sometimes this technique takes the form of the reader meeting the narrator in the present, and then the narrator begins to tell a tale that happened in the past, only to return to the present by the end of the story, drama, or movie. Suspense is thus created because the narrator knows the outcome of the story; so we hold on, waiting to know from the "storyteller" how the conflict will be resolved, how it will come to an end, and how it is that the narrator, or chief protagonist, came to be telling us this story in his or her present circumstances. *Revenge dramas,* for example, often start out with the chief protagonist remembering with pain the story of the murder of his family, friends, or other significant persons, and then lead forward to the climax of his or her revenge, usually bringing us to the climactic moment in which he or she is about to consummate his or her revenge in the "present." This is the sort of plot device that keeps the reader paying attention because he or she wants to know what happens next.

5.3 Characters/Methods of Characterization

Without characters, fictional plots in drama and fiction could not take place. Characters are the "people" of the virtual, or "second" universe in the "slice of life" that the author lets the reader see. Most fictions and dramas have *protagonists,* or the main characters who are at the center of the action and the story, and *antagonists,* those who struggle against the protagonist in the conflict presented in the story or drama. Characters can be of many types, but there are some fundamental *methods of characterization* that writers use over and over again with great variations.

The writer uses two general methods for characterization. Characters can be either *flat,* or *round (three-dimensional).* Those who have a single overriding quality (such as the Hare in Aesop's fable) and never change or develop in the course of a story or drama are considered *flat characters.* *Flat characters* are also those associated with fairy tales, romances, and allegories, where they are always representative of a quality or an idea and lack true individuality. In the "Grasshopper and the Ant," the ant represents patience, hard work, and industry, and the grasshopper represents frivolousness, recklessness, and irresponsibility. Neither of them changes from the beginning of the fable until the end. That is their purpose and their role.

Round or *three-dimensional characters* are those who show a complex variety of qualities and attributes and are "human" through and through—full of failures and successes. *Round characters* change and develop in the course of the story or drama and demonstrate an individuality, sometimes within a type; thus, Huckleberry Finn is styled after the type of flat character called a *picaro,* or orphan, who makes it in the "school of hard knocks" and survives by his wits. But Huck, although he fits this type, also has his individuality and his own rough opinions of things, making him a much more interesting character than just an example of a type.

In addition to depicting characters by type or individuality, writers who use *round* characters show them develop, from bad to worse, from good to bad, from bad to better, or from bad to good. Comedies usually show characters who develop from bad to good or from good to better, while tragedies usually depict characters who go from good to bad or from good to bad and back to good by having suffered some unchangeable and uncontrollable setback from which they cannot recover. Thus, Oedipus in *Oedipus Rex* finds out too late that he has killed his father, married his mother, and brought a plague upon Thebes, the city that he had saved from the Sphinx by solving the famous riddle years before.

Usually, however, tragic characters show some degree of nobility in the face of overwhelming odds: for example, ethical strength, courage, or unconditional love. Varieties are only as limited as the authors who create them. The tragic hero usually must overcome or deal with what the ancient Greeks called *hubris,* or overwhelming arrogance and pride in the face of the gods or fate. Usually, the gods or fate win and humble the arrogant hero in the course of time by the end of the play or fiction.

In addition to using individuals and types, writers use other more immediate methods to develop or reveal their characters, natures, and personalities. Characters are revealed to the reader or viewer through several specific qualities and devices: *their looks* (their manner of dress; their height; their deformities, scars, or hairstyles; what kind of habits they reveal), *their words v. their deeds, and how other characters in the same story view them in the context of the story or play.* A "portrait" then emerges of the character in question, based on these ways of observing who or what they are.

5.3.1 Heroes and Antiheroes

A special form of protagonist, known as the *hero* or *heroine,* has changed greatly since the beginning of extant literature in the West. Aristotle's guidelines for the hero are as follows: a man of noble or high birth, a king or aristocrat; a man of noble intention and with high ethical and intellectual skills; a man of great courage and high purpose. This *heroic type* did not include women, except as adjuncts or relatives of the hero. Gradually, this concept of the hero began to change.

The chief change comes with the Renaissance in Europe, when heroes who had fewer of these qualities started to appear. In particular, in Spain, a chief protagonist appeared who had none of these qualities—they were all the opposite: the *picaro*. The Renaissance began to move away from accepted types in literature toward more individual and personable heroes. In fact, the *picaro* actually emerged as the direct opposite of the traditional hero and became the *antihero*. Since then, many changes have occurred. What is important to remember is that a *chief protagonist could now have any of the qualities from the high noble to the low criminal and still be the main driving force behind the action and/or narrative of the story at hand.*

5.3.2 Stock Characters and Stereotypes

Over the course of time, a number of characters appear over and over again in literature. Some are so well known that they have become *stereotypes,* or stock characters, who have lost their individuality and are only important as minor, flat characters who support the main characters in moving the action forward. For example, in a western, the stock character, or stereotype, of the confiding bartender at the local saloon who lets the hero know where the "gang of bank robbers" is meeting to plan their deed.

Some of these characters have been mentioned previously in Chapter 2, but some deserve special mention because they appear over and over again. Some characters are used *ironically* as stereotypes who turn out not to be what they seem to be. For example, some writers use the hero as some form of "the knight in shining armor"—who looks good, talks a good story, comes from a good family, and even has intelligence and courage, but who turns out to be an evil, ugly, vicious criminal in his internal character and personality despite his outward trappings. Sometimes this is a cowboy in a western; sometimes it is a businessman, a doctor or the like. The reverse is also sometimes true—the character appears rough, of low birth, and even stupid (as with Benjy in Faulkner's *The Sound and the Fury),* but turns out to be deep in his or her soul, excellent, upright, and righteous.

Problem Solving Example:

Q Read the passage below carefully. Then write an essay explaining the narrator's attitude toward the "speaker" and analyzing the technique the narrator uses to define the "speaker's" character.

"Now, what I want is Facts. Teach these boys and girls nothing but Facts. Facts alone are wanted in life. Plant nothing else, and root out everything else. You can only form the minds of reasoning animals upon Facts: nothing else will ever be of any service to them. This is the principle on which I bring up my own children, and this is the principle on which I bring up these children. Stick to Facts, sir!"

The scene was a plain, bare, monotonous vault of a school-room, and the speaker's square forefinger emphasized his observations by underscoring every sentence with a line on the schoolmaster's sleeve. The emphasis was helped by the speaker's square wall of a forehead, which had his eyebrows for its base, while his eyes found commodious cellarage in two dark caves, overshadowed by the wall. The emphasis was helped by the speaker's voice, which was inflexible, dry, and dictatorial. The emphasis was helped by the speaker's hair, which bristled on the skirts of his bald head, a plantation of firs to keep the wind from its shining surface, all covered with knobs, like the crust of a plum pie, as if the head had scarcely warehouse-room for the hard facts stored inside. The speaker's obstinate carriage, square coat, square legs, square shoulders—nay, his very neckcloth, trained to take him by the throat with an unaccommodating grasp, like a stubborn fact, as it was—all helped the emphasis.

"In this life, we want nothing but Facts, sir; nothing but Facts!"

The speaker, and the schoolmaster, and the third grown person present, all backed a little, and swept with their eyes the inclined pane of little vessels then and there arranged in order, ready to have imperial gallons of facts poured into them until they were full to the brim.
From *Hard Times* by Charles Dickens

 A This Answer provides three sample essays that represent possible responses to the essay topic. Compare your own response to those given on the next few pages. Allow the strengths and weaknesses of the sample essays to help you critique your own essay and improve your writing skills.

SAMPLE ESSAY: Well-written

In this passage, the narrator's attitude towards the speaker is unsympathetic. The narrator draws a portrait of a stuffy, straight-edged, no-deviation-from-the-facts, knows-everything kind of man. This is a man who cannot see any beauty in life. He has pushed all the fascination and mystery out of life, and replaced it with facts. So many facts are inside him, he looks as though he is going to burst.

The narrator observes, "The speaker's square forefinger emphasized his observations by underscoring every sentence with a line on the schoolmaster's sleeve." The way the speaker uses his mind there is one set of rules that he lives by and he has no intention of deviating from them. He means every word he speaks with all his being.

The narrator makes wonderful use of the word "square." It is used to describe the speaker's finger, the "square wall" of his forehead, his "square coat," "square legs," and "square shoulders." It creates a clear picture of a person, chiseled out of rock, no roundness to him, no softness. He is just a hard, straight-path, all facts kind of man. This impression is further developed by the phrases the narrator uses to describe the speaker's eyes: "while his eyes found commodious cellarage in two dark caves, overshadowed by the wall." No smile or twinkle will ever find their way into this man's eyes.

The narrator describes the speaker's voice as "dry, inflexible and dictatorial," as is perfectly suitable for a man of facts. The speaker's neckcloth has him by the throat in an "unaccommodating grasp," as if to show that should he somehow let a nonfact slip out, it would strangle him.

Ironically, the narrator has this man of facts preach his message by using figurative language. The speaker states that, "Facts alone are wanted in life. Plant nothing else, and root out everything else." Even he cannot stick to the facts to describe the importance of facts. This detail tells us that the narrator detests this prophet of facts.

The narrator's portrait of the speaker is unflattering and critical. The narrator has achieved this effect through his repetition of the word "square," the details describing his eyes and his voice, and the ironic placement of figurative language in the mouth of a man of facts. He is, in short, an emotionless automaton.

ANALYSIS

This essay accurately interprets the narrator's attitude toward the speaker in the passage. It reveals a perceptive understanding of the narrator's deliberate undercutting of the speaker's credibility as a man of fact by salting his speech with figurative language. There is a thorough discussion of the narrator's use of the word "square" and the psychological portrait it creates. The writer could have devoted more time to analyzing Dickens's images, such as the cumulative effect created by the repetition of sentences beginning with the phrase, "The emphasis was helped" being made about the speaker's eyes and his neckcloth. The writer demonstrates stylistic maturity through the effective listing of descriptors in sentence two. On the whole the writing displays an effective command of sentence structure, diction and organization.

SAMPLE ESSAY: Satisfactory

In this passage, the narrator paints the speaker as a stuffy, strait-edge, by-the-book, know-it-all man. The speaker cannot see any beauty in life. He has removed all the mystery and fascination from life and replaced it with facts. With so many facts inside of him, the speaker looks as if he is going to bust.

The narrator observes, "The speaker's square forefinger emphasized his observations by underscoring every sentence with a line on the school master's sleeve." This shows how the speaker uses his mind: He lives by one set of rules and has no intention of deviating from them. In his heart, he believes every word he speaks.

The narrator emphasizes the word "square" in his description of the speaker. It is used to describe the speaker's finger, the "square wall" of his forehead, his "square coat," and "square shoulders." It creates a picture of a man made of rock with no roundness or softness to him. He is hard, straight-path, an all facts type of man. This view is further developed by the phrases the narrator uses to describe the speaker's eyes: "While his eyes found commodious cellarage in two dark caves, overshadowed by the walls." This man will never smile, and there will be no twinkle in his eyes.

The narrator describes the speaker's voice as suitable for a man of facts. It is "dry, inflexible and dictatorial." The speaker's neckcloth has an "unaccommodating grasp" around his throat. If the man spoke a nonfact, his neckcloth would strangle him.

In a twist of irony, the narrator has the man give his message using figurative language. The speaker states, "Facts alone are wanted in life. Plant nothing else, and root out everything else." This tells readers the narrator dislikes the profit of facts.

The narrator's portrait of the speaker is in unflattering and critical. This is achieved through the narrator's repetition of the word "square," the details describing the speaker's eyes and voice, and the speaker using figurative language. Hence, the narrator sees the speaker as emotionless.

ANALYSIS
In this essay, which is a character sketch, the introduction shows that the writer will describe the narrator's perception of the character, rather than just the character himself. The narrator sees the speaker as a stuffy, straight-edge, by-the-book man who is obsessed with facts. The introduction contains two word choice errors ("strait" should be "straight" and "bust" should be "burst").

The next paragraph, which focuses on the speaker's state of mind, begins the body of the essay. It is illustrated with examples from the book itself, for instance, the "speaker's square forefinger [which] emphasized his observations by underscoring every sentence on the schoolmaster's sleeve." Despite the references from the book, the writer does not substantiate every argument put forth in the paragraph. The statement, "In his heart, he believes every word he speaks," seems to be the essay writer's opinion, and no evidence is provided to support it.

The second body paragraph focuses of the significance of the word "square." The writer shows how the narrator uses it to describe the speaker's finger, forehead, coat, and shoulders. The narrator explains that the speaker is a man made of rock, who is characterized as being "hard." This is illustrated by a narrator's reference to the speaker's eyes as 'two dark caves, overshadowed by the wall.' Once again, although the references are helpful in reinforcing the writer's argument, they are not very well linked to the book itself, or, indeed, to the rest of the essay.

The next body paragraph, which focuses on the speaker's voice and on the significance of his neckcloth, contains interesting observations, but it is not enough to merely restate images from the essay. It would be far more helpful to draw a conclusion based on the examples taken from the book—to help us see something more in it than we might see from our own reading.

The final body paragraph focuses on the speaker's use of figurative language, which the essay writer calls a "twist of irony." To notice that this man, so obsessed with facts, uses figurative language, is a very good insight. However, the paragraph is not carefully constructed or well-developed. This, in combination with the error in word choice makes the paragraph confusing, and obscures the cleverness of the point being made. The paragraph contains one word choice error ("profit" should be "prophet").

The writer organized the character sketch very well. However, lack of development, confusing language, and the three word choice errors detract from the essay's strengths. With a little revision this could become quite a good essay.

SAMPLE ESSAY: Unsatisfactory

In this passage, the narrator has no sympathy toward the speaker. The narrator views the speaker as a stuffy, straight-edged, all facts, know-it-all kind of man. The speaker sees no beauty in life. He lives by facts there is no fascination or mystery in his life. With all these facts inside him. He looks like he is going to burst.

The narrator observes the image of the "square" in the speaker. The speaker lives by one set of rules and dopes not deviate from them.

The narrator continues his discussion of the "square," relating it to the speaker's body. The narrator paints the speaker as a man chiseled out of stone with no roundness or softness in him. This image is further developed in the narrator's description of the speaker's eyes: "While his eyes found no commodious cellarage in two dark caves overshadowed by the wall." This man's eyes will never twinkle or smile.

The narrator describes the speaker's vioce as "dry, inflexible, and dictatorial." According to the narrator, this suits the speaker. The narrator also notes that speaker's neckcloth fits him tightly. If a nonfact slipped out, the speaker would be strangled by his neckcloth.

In a twist of irony, the narrator has this man of facts preach his message using figurative language. The narrator goes on to say that even this man cannot stick to facts to describe facts. This detail lets the reader know the narrator is not fond of the speaker.

The narrator paints an unflattering and critical picture of the speaker. This is achieved through the repetition of the word "square," the description of the speaker's voice and eyes, and the speaker's use of figurative language. In conclusion, this man of facts is without emotion.

ANALYSIS

This essay is an analysis of a character sketch. From the first paragraph, or introduction, the sentences are clipped and insufficient to convey all that the writer wishes to say. This paragraph contains one run-on sentence ("He lives by facts there is no fascination or mystery in his life") and one sentence fragment ("With all these facts inside him.")

Throughout the body of the essay the writer does not adequately develop his or her ideas. Nor does he or she give examples from the passage. Furthermore, the writer does not connect observations based on the passage to conclusions drawn from these observations, which causes the opinions that are set forth to feel vague and unsupported. It would be advisable to expand the paragraphs so that the ideas flow more comfortably together, and so that every idea that is introduced is fully explored.

This essay is not carefully organized, and it lacks development and supporting examples in most paragraphs. Furthermore, grammatical and mechanical errors are frequent enough to mar the quality of this essay.

5.4 Dialogue

Dialogue is the talk with which characters in a fiction or in a drama engage one another. Dialogue serves two main purposes: to move the action of the play or fiction forward, and to reveal the thoughts of a particular character. Many writers use colloquial language, dialect, and other devices to indicate a character's education, ethical interest, and other ways of seeing the world. Some authors use a special form of dialogue known as *internal monologue,* which reveals the innermost thoughts of their characters. James Joyce takes this technique to one of its limits when he uses *internal monologue* to allow the character Molly Bloom to think in a stream of consciousness. *Stream of consciousness* is a literary technique in which a character's thoughts are characterized by a manner in which they are presented as occurring in random form, without regard for logical sequences.

5.5 Figurative Language and Tone: Image, Metaphor, Symbol, and Myth

Figurative language in fiction, drama, or poetry, not only uses connotations to evoke mood and help characterize an actor or character, but is often used to point to or suggest by implication larger themes to the reader. For example, Huck Finn visits many cities along the Mississippi, one of which is Goshen, by which Mark Twain may invoke a comparison or analogy between Huck's journey down the river and the Biblical journey to the City of Goshen. *Archetypal patterns,* or recurring literary themes, images, and plots, first noticed by the psychologist Carl Jung, are often used by writers to promote comparisons or analogies between the problems of the characters in the immediate work and all humanity. These patterns (often called *motifs*) suggest connections with others. Some of these patterns, along with other standard forms, will be discussed below.

5.5.1 Images

Images are rarely used for their own sake in a good work of art. An *image* is sensory and tangible and may be any sight, sound, smell, taste, or physical feeling that a writer may use to generate a pervasive mood or tone. For example, to evoke the hot, busy mood of the New York City streets in summer, a writer may bring in the sounds of horns and other street noise, the smells of food, the actual temperature, the greasy feel of clothes or tools, the colors of objects in the environment, and so on.

One special form of image that writers have begun to use is an intellectual image, called a *literary* or *historical allusion*. The writer may allude or refer to anything in the public record—science, art, literature, music, and so on—in an effort to have the reader associate the character or situation with that history, knowledge, or idea. For example, in his famous poem, "The Love Song of J. Alfred Prufrock," T.S. Eliot alludes to the famous Italian Renaissance sculptor Michelangelo to heighten, by way of contrast, the genius sculptor with the sense of the superficial and petty world in which Prufrock exists: Prufrock says,

> In the rooms,
> The women come and go,
> Talking of Michelangelo …

5.5.2 Metaphors and Similes

Metaphors and similes are used by writers to show relationships between situations or characters in drama, fiction, and poetry that point to larger issues and themes and to create a mood. A *metaphor* is the linking together of two items not usually associated, the combination of which suggests an identity between them that does not exist in real life, but which has the force of truth or feeling. For example, "Life is a journey through a dark wood," suggests that going on in life is like taking a journey through a dark forest. This identity between the two unlike or otherwise unrelated ideas is a metaphor that evokes a mood of dread and of the unknown. The metaphoric comparison brings up fears of what lies ahead on "the path of life."

Metaphors can take many forms: *auditory* ("the fear sounded a bell in my heart"), evoking memories of sound linked to an emotion; *olfactory* ("death is a fermenting, rancid cheese..."), evoking a relationship between an idea and the sense of smell; *visual* ("death is a red sunset"), evoking something seen coupled with an idea; *tactile* ("the nails of his fear dug into his hands..."), coupling an idea with something touched; *savory* ("the warm bread of his feelings for her..."); or *tensile* ("the responsibility was a stretched band in his gut..."), evoking bodily muscular tension. In all cases, the author links an image to an idea which may be another image, thing, or person, to evoke a thought greater than the sum of its parts.

Metaphors sometimes take a special linguistic form known as a *simile* in which the writer compares two or more ideas and uses the words "like" or "as" to make the comparison or analogy. For example, here are two *similes:*

"Jeannie was as worried *as a long-tailed cat* in a room full of rocking chairs."

"George raised his hand *like a hammer* over the fallen gangster."

Symbols in literature are usually concrete objects that stand for or represent an abstraction. *Symbols* in literature are not always things. Sometimes characters become *symbolic,* especially in allegories, fables, and romances, where they may represent whole ideas such as Truth or Beauty. In some of the early "passion plays" of medieval Europe, characters were named for Christian figures. Christ might be called "the Lamb," for "the lamb of God." Or a character who stands for all humankind might be called Everyman so that viewers would be sure to know that for which he stood. In Marjorie Kinnan Rawlings's *The Yearling,* it might be said that the yearling deer represents Innocence, so that when the animal has to die, the young male protagonist "loses" his "innocence."

Symbols, like metaphors and images, allow readers or viewers to understand a work of literature at a different level than the literal. Figurative language allows the reader or viewer to raise the story from merely a story to possible universal applications to the human condition. It is through figurative language that literature acquires its "deeper meanings." The student's job is to analyze the figurative language with a view to showing how those metaphors, symbols, and images support the theme or convey some deeper meaning than just the literal events of the story itself.

5.5.3 Myths and Mythologies

Myths and mythologies are the crowning combination of a story told through images, metaphors, and symbols of the deepest cultural beliefs of a people or civilization. *Myths* have, for some people, the negative connotation of being "untrue stories" or "unbelievable tales." But these are corrupt and superficial meanings of the term. *Myths* are the stories that a people or civilization holds dear, and they reflect the mores, norms, and other social values held by that civilization.

The Greek myths that often depict the conflict between the gods and humans reflect much about the values that the ancient Greeks held sacred. Courage and knowledge were very important to the Greeks. For example in their mythology, there is the story of a daring and proud young man named Prometheus. Prometheus is the man who gave humans the knowledge of how to use fire. He made a deal with Zeus (the God of all the gods), and acquired the knowledge of how to start and use fire, under the condition that he wouldn't give that knowledge to his fellow humans. However, he did give away this knowledge (showing great courage in defying the gods). For this, Zeus punished Prometheus and had him live forever chained to an exposed mountain rock where each day an eagle came and ate out his liver. Prometheus's liver was restored each day, only to have him suffer the pain of having it eaten again and again.

This "myth" is not a lie; it is a made-up story. It didn't actually happen in reality, but Prometheus's story is one with a thousand human analogies. How often have humans "defied the gods" only to "pay" some eternal "price" for the "knowledge?" For example, Oppenheimer and others learned to split the atom and unleash the enormous power of the atomic bomb (the knowledge from "the gods"), but the price of that knowledge was the need for a new "eternal" vigilance to prevent the possible wholesale destruction of the Earth and everyone in it.

The student's job is to see if a given author uses *literary or mythic allusions* with images, metaphors, and symbols to refer to or remind the audience of the similarity or contrast between his or her fiction or drama and a well-known cultural myth, thereby enlarging the scope or deepening the meaning of what is happening in a given story or play.

5.5.4 Allegory and Romance

Allegory and romance are special forms of storytelling that deserve mention here. *Novels* are long works of fiction that can imitate real life and are set in the present (Updike's *Rabbit Run,* Styron's *Sophie's Choice),* the known historical past (Crane's *The Red Badge of Courage* set in the Civil War), or the imagined future (Clarke's *2001). Novels* began to take precedence over other forms of literature as the Industrial Revolution came about. The works of Dickens *(Oliver Twist, David Copperfield),* Jane Austen *(Pride and Prejudice),* and George Eliot/ Mary Ann Evans *(Silas Marner, Middlemarch)* are exemplary. Novels are about realistic characters in realistic settings of time and place.

Allegories and *romances,* however, are set in timeless places and unreal or idealized settings *(Beauty and the Beast, King Arthur and the Knights of the Round Table, The 1001 Arabian Nights),* and tend to have an air of timelessness and distance. The hackneyed opening of a child's "fairy tale" is emblematic of how romances strike a tone: "Once upon a time in a land far, far away, there lived a ..." In romances and allegories, the characters tend to be flat and do not develop much, except perhaps to overturn the villain. Characters in allegories are never ironic, they are always what they appear to be and are sometimes named as such. Consider the following common allegorical melodrama:

Mr. Right meets Miss Innocence and they fall in love. The evil banker, named Mr. Greedyone, appears and tries to fore-close on Miss Innocence's mother's home, called HomeSweet. Mr. Greedyone says, however, that if Mrs. Goodmother will give Miss Innocence's hand in marriage to him, he will tear up the mortgage. But Mrs. Goodmother (Miss Innocence's mom), knowing this is not right, turns to Mr. Right for help. And sure enough, through hard work, Mr. Right finds the money in time to save Mrs. Goodmother's home and foil Mr. Greedyone's plan to get HomeSweet and Miss Innocence. Miss Innocence turns to Mr. Right with love in her eyes and says, "My hero!" And they all "live happily ever after."

Allegories are rarely subtle, and though the characters' names might not be this obvious, their deeds and their roles always match their allegorical names (Mr. Greedyone might instead, for example, be called Mr. Moneybags, but the effect would be the same). These stories and tales, since they are vehicles for the dramatic presentation of ideas, usually dramatically depict the working out of some moral. In this case, we might say the moral of the story is that *love conquers all.*

Aesop's fables are allegorical and demonstrate another device: *personification.* Personification is that device in which *a writer turns an idea, object, or feeling into a living being.* Personification is one of the most widely used literary devices. It is this device that makes dogs capable of speech and feeling as in *The Lady and the Tramp* cartoon or in one of the most famous personifications ever, that of the dog Buck in *The Call of the Wild,* a novel by Jack London that is told completely from Buck's point of view. Other examples include having trees with voices and faces (as in *The Wizard of Oz),* mirrors that can talk back to you, or where the young heroine is the *personification of beauty.* Allegories have largely lost their appeal to modern audiences except as children's stories or futuristic science fantasy.

Romances, which are often timeless, are nevertheless often set in a familiar setting, though no particular time is named. Romances are often, but not always, about thwarted or illicit love. The keys to an effective romance are emotionally grand characters doing grand and daring deeds in exotic and turbulent settings, and these stories can be found on any drugstore bookstand in America (with a cover that usually shows a barely clothed woman being "swept off her feet" by an equally ill-clad youth in some violent storm on a ship at sea, on a faraway island, or in a grand castle or mansion). They are still a much-read and much-loved genre, though their contribution to the growth of the literary form has fundamentally ceased.

Problem Solving Example:

Q Read the following poem carefully. Then write an essay in which you analyze how the poet employs images of nature to support his central theme. Develop your essay with specific references to the text of the poem.

The Wind and the Rain
I
That far-off day the leaves in flight
Were letting in the colder light.
A season-ending wind that blew
That, as it did the forest strew,
5 I leaned on with a singing trust
And let it drive me deathward too.
With breaking step I stabbed the dust,
Yet did not much to shorten stride.
I sang of death—but had I known
10 The many deaths one must have died
Before he came to meet his own!
Oh, should a child be left unwarned
That any song in which he mourned
Would be as if he prophesied?
15 It were unworthy of the tongue
To let the half of life alone
And play the good without the ill.
And yet 'twould seem that what is sung

In happy sadness by the young,
20 Fate has no choice but to fulfill.

II

Flowers in the desert heat
Contrive to bloom
On melted mountain water led by flume
To wet their feet.
25 But something in it still is incomplete.
Before I thought the wilted to exalt
With water I would see them water-bowed.
 I would pick up all ocean less its salt,
And though it were as much as cloud could bear
30 Would load it onto cloud,
And rolling it inland on roller air,
Would empty it unsparing on the flower
That past its prime lost petals in the flood
(Who cares but for the future of the bud?),
35 And all the more the mightier the shower
Would run in under it to get my share.

'Tis not enough on roots and in the mouth,
But give me water heavy on the head
In all the passion of a broken drouth.

40 And there is always more than should be said.

As strong as rain without as wine within,
As magical as sunlight on the skin.

I have been one no dwelling could contain
When there was rain;
45 But I must forth at dusk, my time of day,
To see to the unburdening of skies.
Rain was the tears adopted by my eyes
That have none left to stay.

A   This Answer provides three sample essays that represent possible responses to the essay topic. Compare your own response to those given on the next few pages. Allow the strengths and weaknesses of the sample essays to help you critique your own essay and improve your writing skills.

SAMPLE ESSAY: Well-written

In "The Wind and the Rain," poet Robert Frost effectively uses images from nature to support his central theme: that man, like the creatures of nature, needs to be refreshed by the life forces around him, even if they may be dangerous to his frail human form.

The poem opens with a self-description of the poet in old age—lost, as it were, in a forest of strewn leaves and "season-ending" wind. In an almost biblical death reference, the poet stabs the dust and sings of "death." Perhaps, he muses, it would have been better for himself and for other humans if we did not contemplate death before it actually happened-if we did not walk mournfuly through the empty forest expecting our end.

In the second section, the speaker describes the manner in which a desert flower attempts to bloom even among the harsh surrounding conditions. This is the force of life that is transmuted by animating water which can revive the wilted, and even, we are led to speculate, the almost-dead. The speaker, of course, expresses his fondness for water "as much as cloud could bear." If he had his way, he would give as much as he could to the desert flower, and as much as he could to himself, or, as he says "give me water heavy on the head / In all the passion of a broken drouth."

It is possible that the water represents his lost youth, and that the poet's desire for "strong rain" and increasing need to search it out at "dusk, my time of day," is a reminder to him that he is approaching old age and should absorb as much of life as possible, even if it is uncomfortable or dangerous for him to do so. That the speaker has "dried out" like the desert flower, is underscored by the poet's last observation: he needs the rain because his eyes no longer tear. If they did, one suspects the tears would be for his own imminent departure from life.

Using images of desert, forest, and sky, Frost artfully weaves a fabric of images—both of nature and of himself—that support his poem's central theme about man' s hunger to retrieve life even as he confronts his leaving it.

ANALYSIS

This essay is well written. It demonstrates the writer's command of syntax, organization, and diction, and effectively describes how the poet uses images from nature to support his central theme. Notice how the writer gives examples of both images and theme, and how he uses them to clearly and directly answer the question.

SAMPLE ESSAY: Satisfactory

In "The Wind and the Rain," Robert Frost uses images from nature to support his theme: Man, like the creatures of nature, needs to be refreshed by the life forces around him, even if these forces may be dangerous to his health.

The poem begins with a the poet describing himself in old age. He sees himself lost in a forest of fallen leaves and "season-ending" wind. In an almost biblical reference, the poet stabs the dust and sings of "death." He jokes that it would have been better if we did not think about death before it happens and that we should not walk in an empty forest expecting death.

In the second section, Frost describes the way a desert flower tries to bloom in harsh surroundings. The force of life is transformed by animating water to revive the wilted and the almost dead. The speaker is fond of water. If he could, he would give the flower and himself the same amount of water.

To Frost, water represents his lost youth. His desire for a "strong rain" and need to search out "dusk, my time of day" reminds him that he is getting old and should actively participate in life, even if it kills him. The speaker says that he had dried out like the desert flower. Frost says he needs the rain because his eyes not being able to tear. He fears if the tears came, they would signal his death.

Frost uses images of nature and himself to support his theme: Man is hungry to retrieve life even as he confronts death.

ANALYSIS

The essay begins with the name of the poem (Robert Frost's "The Wind and the Rain"), and then presents the thesis statement, which is that Robert Frost " ...uses images from nature to support his central theme: Man, like the creatures of nature, needs to be refreshed by the life forces around him, even if these forces may be dangerous to his health." This paragraph is only one sentence long, and this is not usually an adequate length to develop an idea that will be explored in a full-length essay. It is helpful not merely to state what will be discussed in the essay, but to explain and develop it to such an extent that it can support the remainder of the essay.

The next paragraph starts the essay's body. In the paragraph's first sentence, the word "begins" indicates that the essay writer will elaborate on the poem's first part, in which Frost describes himself as an old man. The essay writer uses examples from the poem, such as "season-ending wind," to support the discussion. This paragraph leads awkwardly into the next paragraph, in which the writer explains the significance of the desert flower. The paragraph lacks a transition, so the reader assumes that the writer is still addressing part one of the poem, rather than part two.

In the final paragraph, or conclusion, the writer reminds the reader of the essay's central theme: Man yearns for life as he faces death. Once again, the brevity of this paragraph, and the awkwardness with which it is written, weaken it. It is important to have a strong conclusion in order to unify all of the ideas explored in the paper. Throughout this essay, in fact, more careful use of language and a more thorough examination of ideas would have yielded a more well-written paper.

SAMPLE ESSAY: Unsatisfactory

In "The Wind and the Rain," Robert Frost uses images of nature to support his theme. His theme is man needs to be refreshed by the life forces around him even if they may be dangerous to his health.

Frost begins by describing himself in old age. He is lost is a forrest of fallen leaves and "season-ending" wind. Almost Biblical reference. Frost stabs the dust and sings of death. He laughs at himself and at other people who think of death before it happens.

In the second section, he describes a desert flower. Attempts to bloom in harsh conditions. This is the force of life that is transmuted by animating water which can revive the wilted and the almost-dead. The speaker is fond of water and says that he would give as much as he could to the desert flower.

Water represents the speaker's lost youth. His desire for "strong rain" and need to search it out at "dusk, my time of day" is a remainder that he is growing old and should live life to the fullest. The speaker says he is "dried out" like the desert flower; he needs the rain because his eyes can no longer tear. If he cried, he suspects it would be for his own death.

Using images of the desert, forest, and sky, the poet skillfully weaves images of himself and nature to support his poem's central theme: Man yearns to retrieve life as he confronts leaving it.

ANALYSIS

The first paragraph, or introduction, lacks a strong statement of purpose. The phrase "his theme" is redundant, as it ends the first sentence and begins the second sentence. These sentences should be joined in order to make the essay's statement of purpose stronger.

The second paragraph begins the body of the essay. The essay writer supports his/her views with examples from the poem—"fallen leaves," "season-ending wind," "stabs the dust," and "sings of death." The paragraph contains a fragment ("Almost Biblical reference"), a capitalization error ("Biblical" should not be capitalized), and a spelling error ("forrest" should be "forest"). In paragraphs three and four, the writer speaks of the significance of the desert flower, but does not provide adequate development for this point. The fourth paragraph explains that water represents the poet's lost youth, and the writer's views are supported by examples from the poem—"dusk, my time of day" and "dried out." These paragraphs contain several grammatical and mechanical errors—a sentence fragment ("Attempts to bloom in harsh conditions"), and a word choice error ("Remainder" should be "reminder").

The conclusion restates the essay's purpose. Its renames the images used in the poem (desert, forest, and sky) and reminds the reader of the essay's major point: Man wants life in the face of death. This paragraph could have been expanded to give a stronger finish to the essay. In fact, the lack of a strong statement of purpose and the fact that supporting information is missing throughout the paper weaken this essay. Also contributing to this essay's faults are the writer's mechanical and grammatical errors.

5.6   Archetypal Patterns and Common Themes in Literature

Literary works often show the recurrence of common themes and common situations. Some of these have been touched upon above. The psychologist Carl Jung, among others, has noted how these reappear in literature over and over. These *archetypal patterns,* when revealed in a work of literature, serve to frame the fiction on a mythic level or just help the student to understand the fundamental themes at play in the work in question. Psychologists and literary historians believe that these patterns appear because they are fundamental to the human condition and that literature brings them before us in a myriad of variations relevant to our time and place, and yet still the same patterns.

5.6.1   Person Against Person, Nature, Society, or God (or the gods)

Most literature depicts one or another of these classic conflicts and will resolve them or not depending upon the intent of the author. Stories of rival kings or queens and person against person; science fiction stories about a woman defeating a grossly sociopathic organism never before encountered by science, as depicted by Sigourney Weaver against the Alien in the movie of that name (woman against

Nature); epic poems about an uncommonly heroic warrior king over-coming the power of the gods to have his way (Odysseus in the an-cient Greek poet Homer's epic poem *The Odyssey);* or myths about man against the gods which move the human spirit to new awareness of the struggle of human life in a difficult and hostile universe. The best works of literature seem to depict all of these conflicts happen-ing at once, or at least to one life, that of the chief protagonist—hero or antihero—and we are kept wondering how the conflict will be resolved.

5.6.2 Rites of Passage/Literature as the Imitation of Life's "Journey"

Literary critics such as Northrop Frye and others have observed that one way to view literature is not as a series of genres, but as a series of forms that reflect the *archetypal patterns of social and cultural ritu-als.* Literature, in their way of thinking, is a series of analogues for specific *rites of passage* in our culture. A rite of passage is that dra-matic, social ritual that is performed in a culture and is used to mark the onset or change, or "passage," to the next major stage of life. Typically, there are four major rites of passage in most cultures: rituals marking birth, entry into adulthood and the end of adolescence, fertility, and death, or "passage" to some heavenly afterlife. Awareness of such pat-terns by a student critic of literature will add weight to any thesis which might be brought forth about the meaning of a work of literature. A student may, of course, only be called upon to explain or describe the presence of such a pattern or symbolic use of a rite in a paper.

5.6.3 Birth and Rebirth

Authors will often write stories and poems showing that someone is "reborn" into a new and better life after a great struggle—either internal or external—to overcome difficult odds. For example, in Melville's epic novel *Moby Dick,* Ishmael, the narrator, survives the harrowing voyage with Ahab in search of the white whale Moby Dick, and is cast into the sea, only to come back "reborn" as a man with greater insight into the dark workings of a dark universe. Writers often use images such as the sea, nearly drowning, or some other "transfor-mation" to point to a "reborn" spirit or character.

5.6.4 From Adolescence to Adulthood

Some fictions, dramas, and poems are about growing up and becoming a fully successful man or woman. For example, Dickens's *David Copperfield* and *Oliver Twist* show this sort of shift and growth. But, again, an author may use this archetypal pattern or ritual as a backdrop to the action shown. A character, while not really a boy or girl, may move symbolically from an "adolescent" frame of mind into that of a successful "adult" simply by developing from an irresponsible, deadbeat dad to one who pays his bills and shares in the raising of his own abandoned children.

The author might depict such a character in the beginning as concerned about "adolescent" things like looks, peer approval, and clothes to one who matures in concern for others, handling decisions on a personal basis, and nurturing the talents and skills of those around him or her not as fortunate as he or she in the end. The deadbeat dad will thus have symbolically gone through a rite of passage from "adolescence" to "adulthood" by taking a new course of action in his life.

5.6.5 Marriage and Fertility

This rite of passage is legion in literature. It can be used ironically, showing the destruction of a marriage and an "infertile" relationship. This rite is mostly celebrated in musicals, comedies, romances, and soap operas. But the rite may serve as a symbolic backdrop or undercurrent to a story in progress. Thus, a chief protagonist may be "married to his work," making him or her give "birth" to new ideas or a successful marriage, while ironically losing the love of his or her real flesh and blood wife or husband in the process. Sinclair Lewis's famous *Dodsworth* shows just such a situation, when the American businessman who has been "married to his work" takes his wife abroad to Europe and discovers what his false "marriage" has cost him in his real one.

In Shakespeare's *Macbeth,* the reader sees a marriage of real love destroyed by the lust for power, and Lady Macbeth and Macbeth himself complain of their "infertility"—a biological dysfunction symbolic of the "infertile" and "sterile" life to which they are damned by their murderous ways.

5.6.6 Death/Rebirth

Sometimes this rite dominates the literature of horror, as in Bram Stoker's *Dracula* where the ritual of death is overturned by the perverse ritual of vampirism and unholy love. The rite of death becomes ironically turned into the source of eternal life. Death, too, can be used in a symbolic pattern. Thus, novels of psychological horror might depict a man losing his mind and identity in a kind of psychological "death," only to recover and become "alive" again in a new and productive selfhood. This pattern is most often associated with literature about the transformation of the spirit and the soul.

Problem Solving Example:

Q Analyze the following passage from Thoreau's *Walden*. How does the diarist craft his description so that it not only explores symbols of rebirth, but supports the description by the use of effective elements of style, sound, and syntax as well? How is form related to content in Thoreau's passage, entitled "The Green Blade?"

The brooks sing carols and glees to the spring. The marsh hawk, sailing low over the meadow, is already seeking the first slimy life that awakes. The sinking sound of melting snow is heard in all dells, and ice dissolves apace in the ponds. The grass flames up on the hillsides like a spring fire, as if the earth sent forth an inward heat to greet the returning sun; not yellow but green is the color of its flame. The symbol of perpetual youth, the grassblade, like a long green ribbon, streams from the sod, checked indeed by the frost, but anon pushing on again, lifting its spear of last year's hay with the fresh life below. It grows as steadily as the rill oozes out of the ground. It is almost identical with that, for in the growing days of June, when the rills are dry, the grass blades are their channels, and from year to year the herds drink at this perennial green stream and the mower draws from it betlines their winter supply. So our human life but dies down to its root, and still puts forth its green blade to eternity.

—From *Walden,* "The Green Blade."

A This Answer provides three sample essays which represent possible responses to the essay topic. Compare your own response to those given on the next few pages. Allow the strengths and weaknesses of the sample essays to help you critique your own essay and improve your writing skills.

SAMPLE ESSAY: Well-written

Thoreau's passage traces the changing of seasons by the use of symbols that are reinforced by an effective use of appropriate style, sound, and syntax as well.

The author begins his passage with the image of a hawk "seeking the first slimy life that awakes." The earth, therefore, is still asleep under winter's mantle, but already the "sinking sound of melting snow is heard in all dells" and the "ice dissolves." Almost immediately, grass "flames up"—the recognizable first arrival of spring, before flowers bloom and trees grow green with leaves.

Here Thoreau telescopes from an entire "hillside" down to "the grassblade" where his focus remains until the end of the passage. At once he announces it a "symbol of perpetual youth," and, using simile, says that "like a long-green ribbon," it "streams from the sod," even though the change of seasons has not been complete: the frost still appears to "check" it, though it "push[es] on again."

The onomatopoeic "ess" sound throughout the entire passage is emphasized most in this first part of the passage (sing, carols, glees, marsh, sailing, seeking, first slimy, awakes, sinking sound, snow, dells, dissolves, apace, ponds, grass flames, etc.), perhaps to reinforce Thoreau's contention that the sound of spring is the hissing of an essential "spring fire" "flames up like a spring fire," "green is the color of its flame").

The second half of the passage moves from June through the long ("perennial green") stretch of years (periodically checked by the "mower's" harvest) and outward to eternity, because neither oncoming winters nor the mower's seasonal reaping can destroy the roots of the grass blade—which "puts forth its green blade to eternity."

In these concluding lines are two opposing symbols: the grass, the "symbol of perpetual youth," and the "mower," which symbolizes, of course, both approaching winter and an individual's death. To synthesize and emphasize this, Thoreau concludes with the line, "So our human life but dies down to its root, and still puts forth its green blade to eternity." Thus, as the green blade of grass perennially grows from its roots to harvest, and then through the continuing cycles of nature into infinity, Thoreau believes that human lives move from birth through death and into eternity.

ANALYSIS

This extensive response reflects the complex nature of Thoreau's passage, as well as the tightness with which form and content work together here to illustrate a truth of human and general nature. The responder has used a close reading of the text to illustrate the many elements of sound and style that are at work here, and has shaped the essay with attention to the overall argument: that the hope which springs eternal in the natural world operates in humanity's world as well.

SAMPLE ESSAY: Satisfactory

Thoreau uses symbols to indicate the changing of the seasons in this passage. His use of symbols is reinforced by sytle, sound, and syntax.

The passage begins with the image of a hawk "seeking the first slimy life that awakes." The earth is still asleep beneath winter's mantle, but already "the sound of melting snow is felt in all the dells" and "Ice dissolves." Almost immediately, grass "flames up." This is the first recognizable sign of spring.

At this point, Thoreau moves from the entire "hillside" down to the "grass blade" where his focus remains until the end of the passage. Thoreau sees "the grass blade" as a "symbol of perpetual youth." He uses a smile "like a long-green ribbon," it "streams from the sod," yet the changing of the seasons is not complete and frost still appears.

Thoreau uses the onomatopoeic "ess" sound throughout the entire passage. This is emphasized most in the poem's first part. Examples of this include (sing, carols, glees, marsh, sailing, seeking, first slimy, awakes, sinking sound, snow, dells. dissolves, apace, ponds, and grass flames, etc. Using this sound reinforces "fire" ("flames up like a spring fire," "green is the color of the flame").

In the second part of the passage, Thoreau moves from June through the long ("perennial green") stretch of years (periodically checked by the "mower's" harvest) outward to eternity. Neither the oncoming winter nor the mower's seasonal reaping can destroy the roots of the grass blade.

In the final lines the two opposing symbols —"grass," the symbol of perpetual youth and the "mower," the symbol of approaching winter and an individual's death. To emphasize his point, Thoreau concludes with the lines "So our human life but dies down to its root, and still puts forth its green blade to eternity." Thoreau sees the blade of grass as part of nature continuing cycle of going into infinity just like the human life.

ANALYSIS

The introduction to this essay is too brief to adequately present the thesis. It needs to be developed enough to begin to elaborate the subtleties that will be explored throughout the essay, and to motivate the reader to continue with the essay. The paragraph contains one spelling error ("stlye" should be "style").

The body of this paragraph is quite well organized and well developed with examples from the text. It loses strength, however, because of a number of grammatical errors. For instance, there are word choice errors ("shine" should be "sign," "smile" should be "simile") and spelling errors. These errors, combined with a certain choppiness of style caused by short, awkward sentences, make it difficult for the reader to link the ideas presented and understand what the writer is trying to say.

The structure of this essay is very good, but each topic addressed could be covered more completely. Many interesting points are raised, and should be given the attention that they deserve to fully explore their complexities. This, and the fact that the essay has grammatical and mechanical errors, detract from the essay's strength.

SAMPLE ESSAY: Unsatisfactory

In this passage, Thoreau traces the changing of the seasons through the use of symbols, which are supported by style, sound, and syntax.

The passage begins with the image of the flying hawk seeing the first blade of grass coming up through the snow. Thoreau writes the "sinking sound by melting snow is heard all through the dells" and "the ice dissolves." Instantaneously, grass 'flames up': The first sign of spring.

At this point, Thoreau moves from the entire "hillside" to "the grass blade." Thoreau sees grass as a symbol of perpetual youth.

Thoreau emphasizes the onomatopoeic "ess" sound throughout the entire passage. It is used most in the first part.

The passage's second half moves from June through the long stretch of years to eternity. Thoreau feels that neither winter nor mowing can destroy the grass blade.

The concludeing lines use too opposing symbols. They are grass, which symbolizes lasting youth, and the mower, which symbolizes winter is to come and an individual's death. Thoreau ends with the line "So our human life but dies down to its root and still puts forth its green blade to eternity." The blade of grass grows every year from its root to harvest, going through nature's continuous cycle to eternity, just like human life moves from birth to death into eternity.

ANALYSIS

The introduction to this essay, which states that Thoreau's changing of the seasons will be discussed, is too brief to accommodate the complexity of the subject being tackled. A good introduction presents the thesis in such a way that the reader has a basis of knowledge with which to continue the essay. It should also be sufficiently interesting and detailed to provoke the reader to read the rest of the essay.

The second through fifth paragraphs encompass the body of the essay. These paragraphs, which should expand and develop the ideas introduced in the first paragraph, are also too brief to do their job properly. They need to be expanded, and they need concrete examples to support the ideas they explore. The transitions between the paragraphs are awkward and undeveloped. The last paragraph, though fuller than the other paragraphs of the essay, does not effectively conclude the essay. It contains one spelling error ("concludeing" should be spelled "concluding") and one word choice error ("too" should be "two").

The basic structure of this essay is almost satisfactory, but throughout it lacks appropriate development. The writer fails to fully explore each thought, and the transitions from thought to thought are clumsy. The lack of supporting information, together with the multitude of grammatical and mechanical errors also serve to make this essay poorly written.

Quiz: Types of Papers – Writing about Literature

Questions 1-5 are based on the following poem:

DO NOT GO GENTLE INTO THAT GOOD NIGHT

Do not go gentle into that good night,
Old age should burn and rave at close of day;
Rage, rage against the dying of the light.

Though wise men at their end know dark is right,
Because their words had forked no lightning they
Do not go gentle into that good night.

Good men, the last wave by, crying how bright
Their frail deeds might have danced in a green bay,
Rage, rage against the dying of the light.

Wild men who caught and sang the sun in flight,
And learn, too late, they grieved it on its way,
Do not go gentle into that good night.

Grave men, near death, who see with blinding sight
Blind eyes could blaze like meteors and be gay,
Rage, rage against the dying of the light.

And you, my father, there on the sad height,
Curse, bless, me now with your fierce tears, I pray.
Do not go gentle into that good night.
Rage, rage against the dying of the light.

By Dylan Thomas

1. In the first stanza, the poet is addressing

   (A) the general audience.

   (B) wise men, good men, wild men, and grave men.

   (C) older people.

(D)   people of public notoriety.

(E)   "my father."

2.   In the context of the first stanza, lines 2 and 3 express the belief that

(A)   old people should be less complaining.

(B)   old people should vent their anger regularly, and thus prolong their lives.

(C)   old people should fight against death in every way.

(D)   old people should fight against losing the will to live.

(E)   old people should be expected to be bitter and disappointed.

3.   In the second stanza, the poet implies that

(A)   wise men cannot accept death, and so they must protest.

(B)   wise men always knew that their voices could not stop death, and so they accept it.

(C)   no wise person would willingly go gently into death.

(D)   wise men accept the rightness of death, but they protest anyway.

(E)   wise men feel frustrated that they could not expose death to the "light" of the truth they sense.

4.   The "dying of the light" (lines 3, 15, 19) refers metaphorically to

(A)   the passage of time.

(B)   the aging of the body.

(C)   the aging of the spirit.

(D)   death.

(E)   the loss of the will to live.

5.　The use of the word "rage" throughout the poem has the greatest effect in

　　(A)　increasing the emotional intensity of the statement.

　　(B)　providing closure at the end of every stanza.

　　(C)　providing "stock" figures with a vivid emotional reaction.

　　(D)　providing the poet's audience with a clear statement of the poem's message.

　　(E)　reinforcing the "curse" of the last stanza.

Questions 6-10 are based on the following passage:

My daddy's face is a study. Winter moves into it and presides there. His eyes become a cliff of snow threatening to avalanche; his eyebrows bend like black limbs of leafless trees. His skin takes on the pale, cheerless yellow of winter sun; for a jaw he has the edges of a snowbound field dotted with stubble; his high forehead is the frozen sweep of the Erie, hiding currents of gelid thoughts that eddy in darkness. Wolf killer turned hawk fighter, he worked night and day to keep one from the door and the other from under the windowsills. A Vulcan guarding the flames, he gives us proper distribution of heat, lays kindling by, discusses qualities of coal, and teaches us how to rake, feed, and bank the fire. And he will not unrazor his lips until spring.

Winter tightened our heads with a band of cold and melted our eyes. We put pepper in the feet of our stocking, Vaseline on our faces, and stared through dark icebox mornings at four stewed prunes, slippery lumps of oatmeal, and cocoa with a roof of skin.

But mostly we waited for spring, when there could be gardens.

By the time this winter had stiffened itself into a hateful knot that nothing could loosen, something did loosen it, or rather someone.

A someone who splintered the knot into silver threads that tangled us, netted us, made us long for the dull chafe of the previous boredom.

From The Bluest Eye, *by Toni Morrison*

6. It can be inferred from the opening paragraph that

    (A) the narrator's father was a cold and unloving man.

    (B) the house was besieged by wild animals in the winter.

    (C) the narrator's father was strange and alien to his children.

    (D) the narrator's father fought hunger and cold unceasingly.

    (E) the narrator's father was an accomplished hunter.

7. The sentence "My daddy's face is a study" (line 1) is best interpreted to mean that his face

    (A) reflects the formal learning he has acquired.

    (B) reflects the quiet of a study room.

    (C) is an expressive landscape.

    (D) is expressive of his extensive experiences in life.

    (E) is worthy of attention.

8. The phrase "will not unrazor his lips until spring" (line 14) evokes his

    (A) determination to win the battle for survival.

    (B) refusal to shave.

    (C) decision not to shave until spring comes.

    (D) preoccupation with his appearance.

    (E) stern, hostile attitude toward the family.

9.   The image of a "hateful knot" (lines 22-23) is a reference to

   (A)   the poverty of their home.

   (B)   the unspent anger of their father.

   (C)   the boredom of school.

   (D)   the unyielding cold weather.

   (E)   their cold, stiffened muscles.

10.   In context, the phrase "dull chafe" (line 26) is best interpreted to mean

   (A)   the rubbing of winter garments.

   (B)   the discomfort of wearing the same old clothes.

   (C)   the slow passage of time.

   (D)   the absence of new people in their lives.

   (E)   the unvaried rituals of winter life.

ANSWER KEY

1.	(E)	6.	(D)
2.	(C)	7.	(C)
3.	(D)	8.	(A)
4.	(D)	9.	(D)
5.	(A)	10.	(E)

CHAPTER 6

Some Basics about Good Style

6.1 Format

Whether writing about literature or some other topic, professors will expect students to write in standard English with control over style. The student will need to organize the paper in a logical and useful way that supports its purpose. When the student controls the appearance or format of the paper, the paper becomes more accessible to the reader. Students often complain that an English teacher will give them a poor grade and comment that, "My English teacher never even talks about my great ideas!"

Great ideas are not separate from the language with which the writer communicates them. They are written in clear sentences, and they communicate to people quickly, accurately, and without grammatical flaws. Editing style is the key to communicating thoughts.

Papers should not only be well organized, but should also be attractive to the reader's eye. Many word-processing packages have programs to help format correctly. Formatting a paper should be done during the revising stage of the composing process. Review the paper and make changes later, but formatting should be set up before editing, i.e., to control sentence structure, tone, and punctuation.

Format is the way the paper looks to the reader. Usually professors want papers typed on 8½ x 11" unlined paper. They should be typed on one side only, and all the pages should be numbered in the same place on each page. Names, titles, and class identification should be placed where the professor requests them. Typos, or minor typing mistakes, spelling errors, paragraph indentations, and other minor errors in the quality of your copy must be corrected before you hand in your paper.

Most papers are double-spaced, and the right-hand margins are best left naturally uneven, unless the professor directs you to do otherwise. Underlining and *italics* are used mostly for subheadings and to highlight important elements in the text. Be careful to use underlining **bold-face,** and *italics* sparingly; otherwise, they lose their effectiveness.

Paragraphs should be indented a standard five spaces from the left-hand margin. Paragraphs should be kept brief (three or four sentences on average), so as not to tire the reader's eyes with a busy or cluttered look to the page.

Sentences should be varied and relatively brief and should average about 10 to 15 words each. Of course, longer sentences will be written, but sentences that are over 25 words must be read slowly. Sentences that are 30 words or longer usually have to be read twice by the average reader. Make sure that sentences are correct in grammar as well.

Titles of long works, such as novels or histories, are written in *italics.* Titles may also appear underlined. Parts of large works, such as a chapter from a book, or an article in a journal, are cited using quotation marks rather than italics: e.g., "The Rising Cost of Living" might appear in *The Journal of American Economics.* For the formats of particular writing, such as business memos, follow the practices set by the Business, Communications, or English department.

6.2 Diction

Good writing includes controlling *diction* or *choice of words*. Not only does the choice of words reflect intelligence and sophistication, or the lack thereof, but it has an effect on how readers view a writer's ideas. In addition to understanding the *connotations* and *denotations* of words as discussed in Chapter 2, the writer must be careful to use diction that is acceptable to the audience and that observes the standards of *correct usage.*

Be careful not to use slang and other words that are commonly used in conversation. Slang and colloquial expressions are not appropriate in college writing unless they are used for a special rhetorical effect. Of course, vulgar language, including curses, "four-letter words," and obscene expressions of anger are not generally accepted as appropriate language for use in college English. Professors expect college students to learn and to use *Standard English,* that is, English that is accepted as correct and conventional.

Some examples of *slang* include "cool" for "appealing" or "dude" for "man" or "woman." If a student doesn't know whether or not a word is slang or vulgar, consult a dictionary. A good dictionary provides usage labels to identify words as slang or colloquial. Some of the best dictionaries available include the following:

The Random House College Dictionary

The American Heritage Dictionary of the English Language

Webster's New Collegiate Dictionary

Funk & Wagnalls Standard College Dictionary

The Oxford English Dictionary

Longman's Dictionary of American English (helpful for students who are learning English as a second language)

Dialectal expressions, those which are particular to a local area, should be avoided. For example, "Y'all come on down!" is a local expression for "Come visit us!" and while it is not wrong to *say* it, writing it in a formal English essay would be unacceptable.

Wordiness or *using excessive language* in a sentence is frowned upon as a matter of style. Why make the readers read more than they have to? Consider the difference between these two sentences:

(1) Upon disembarkation, I espied with wonder the riches that abounded; whereupon, I immediately politically and militarily overwhelmed the native population.

(2) I came, I saw, I conquered.

The second sentence is recognizable as that spoken by Julius Caesar. Notice how much more powerful and effective the short sentence is and how pompous and wordy the first one is. Here is another example:

(1) In my opinion, I believe and Howard feels that due to the fact that the item was received late, we are not at liberty to accept it.

(2) Howard and I cannot accept the item since we received it too late.

Effective writing is concise and succinct and uses only the words necessary to convey the idea at hand. Useless elaborations that display a large vocabulary are annoying rather than useful or impressive to the reader.

Be careful to avoid *cliches* and *trite expressions* in writing. As George Orwell said in his "Politics and the English Language," you should

> "Never use a metaphor, simile, or other figure of speech which you are used to seeing in print."

Avoid using such "pat" phrases as "cute as a lamb," "pretty as a picture," "strong as an ox," "slept like a log," "in the final analysis," or "flat as a pancake," and the like. These are only a few of the many that come up in conversation. While it might be all right in conversation, cliches are annoying and boring to the reader. *Either eliminate cliches entirely, or find a fresh way to convey the meaning.*

Sexist language, or *language which identifies a social or other role as solely that of one sex* is to be avoided. The following sentence assumes that all employees of the company are male since it uses only the male pronoun to identify them:

"Each employee will receive *his* paycheck in the mail."

The fastest way to resolve this issue is to pluralize the subject:

"All *employees* will receive *their* paychecks in the mail."

Some nouns need to be carefully used when addressing an audience because they sometimes assume only one sex as all inclusive. For example, here are some common nouns that might need to be edited to reflect their audience more truly and correctly:

Inappropriate	Appropriate
authoress	author
cameraman	photographer
guys	people
mankind	people, human beings
fireman	fire fighter
policeman	police officer
salesmen	salespeople
congressmen	members of Congress
chairman	chairperson
spokesman	spokesperson, representative
workmen	workers
mothering, fathering	parenting
coed	student
fatherland, motherland	homeland, native land
sportsmanship	fair play
Mother Nature, Father Time	nature, time
girl Friday	assistant, secretary
man-made	handmade, manufactured

While this list is not exhaustive, it gives an idea of the kinds of words that have become a part of common speech but no longer reflect (and maybe never did) the real nature of the society. Monosexist language is inappropriate unless the group being referred to is actually wholly male or wholly female. Practice using terms and pronouns that reflect a nonsexist or inclusive diction rather than a sexist and exclusive diction.

Exactness of expression is also basic to good style and good diction. The writer should be careful of errors involving *homonyms,* or *words that sound alike but are spelled differently or mean different things.* Here is a list of some common homonyms that are sometimes misused:

affect	effect
bear	bare
breaks	brakes
their	there
attendance	attendants
always	all ways
accept	except
capital	capitol
chose	choose
complement	compliment
principal	principle
discreet	discrete
eminent	imminent

This list is not comprehensive, but a student should try and become familiar with the words that are confusing. Nothing looks more careless or ignorant than misspelled or incorrectly used words. Consider the following sentence:

"John could hardly bare his body's revulsion to taking brakes in the morning."

John is uncomfortable about getting naked to steal the instrument that stops vehicles in motion? The writer should not confuse readers or give them the opportunity to belittle the material written because of carelessness in controlling diction.

Problem Solving Example:

Q Our use of language differs depending upon the manner or conditions in which it is used. Our language may differ in use of syntax, inflection, vocabulary, and pronunciation, dependent on circumstances.

Write an essay describing the differences in the language you would use in two different circumstances—a conversation with a friend and a job interview, for example. Your essay should indicate what purposes the differences in your use of language serve.

A This Answer provides three sample essays which represent possible responses to the essay topic. Compare your own response to those given on the next few pages. Allow the strengths and weaknesses of the sample essays to help you critique your own essay and improve your writing skills.

SAMPLE ESSAY: Well-written

The language I would use in talking to a friend would certainly be different that the language I would use during a job interview. My purpose in both cases would contrast a great deal, and this would be reflected in the ways I spoke. In talking with a friend, I would be informal and not very concerned with such things as showing off my vocabulary or using correct grammar, and I would be more inclined to use slang terms.

My pronunciation and inflection would reflect the common ways that my friends and I speak, reflecting my desire to be casual and "cool." During a job interview I would speak in a more formal vein, to show my potential employer that I am mature and have a firm grasp of the English language.

In talking with a friend, I would be more prone to use phrases drawn from popular culture that we are both aware of. For example, I might say "That's cool," or "That sucks," to make a reference to a popular show on MTV, instead of using such stock phrases as "I like that" or "I'm not fond of that." I would know that my friends and I are members of a group by using such language, since we all know the jokes. I would never use such language during a job interview. Instead I would speak in the clearest language possible in an attempt to show my potential employer that I am intelligent. If s/he were to ask me what I think of school, I wouldn't chuckle and say dismissively, "Sometimes it's cool and sometimes it sucks." I would reflect for a few seconds, and then reply in full sentences, pointing out both the positive and negative aspects of my school—"I enjoy Shakespeare immensely, especially *Macbeth*, but I find chemistry quite challenging sometimes."

In talking with friends I would be more prone to use certain words and phrases, such as "hey," "like," and "you know," in ways that are both unconventional and grammatically incorrect. Upon greeting a friend I would probably address him or her by saying, "Hey man, what's up?" The use of "hey" implies a certain amount of casualness and familiarity, as it is a short monosyllable that rolls off the tongue effortlessly. I would say "man" regardless of the sex of the addressee since among my friends we all understand "man" is an informal way of saying "friend." The final part of my phrase of greeting would be pronounced as one word "whazup." Furthermore my inflection would not rise at the end of this phrase, it would be more of a statement than a question.

In talking with my friends I would pepper my vocabulary with words that have no set meaning on their own, such as "like." "Like" functions as an intensifier, "He was, like, so gone," with emphasis on "like," would imply that the person of whom I was speaking was very, very drunk. I would consciously resist such usage of "like" during a job interview since it is not grammatically correct and it would also show a lack of respect if I were to address my potential employer as if he were one of my peers.

When greeting my interviewer, I would say, in an even tone, "Hello, it's nice to meet you." I would follow this by questioning "How are you?" with a rise in my voice to show that I really want to know how this person is doing. I would continue throughout the interview in this way, being sure that I used my vocabulary in a conventional, intelligent way. I would also make certain that I employed proper grammar during my interview to show my potential employer that I am both respectful and smart.

My use of language among friends would be casual, informal, and idiosyncratic, reflecting these same qualities in our relationships. I would speak properly and formally during a job interview to make a positive impression on the interviewer, and to show him or her that I am an intelligent human being who is capable of communicating clearly and effectively with all people.

ANALYSIS

This well-written essay contrasts the different ways in which one might use language, dependent on circumstances. The opening paragraph clearly states the different purposes that language would serve during a job interview and during a conversation with a friend.

The essay goes on to describe how a conversation with a friend would draw from the vernacular of popular culture. The essay gives concrete examples of such phrases, and points out that the purpose of using them is to form a group identity in which friends feel at ease with each other.

The essay proceeds in a logical way to describe why such language would not be proper during a job interview. The writer of this essay would want to be seen as intelligent during a job interview. The essay states that the way to do this is through the use of full sentences, conventional vocabulary, and correct grammar, of which examples are then given.

The third, fourth, and fifth paragraphs of this essay contrast the use of pronunciation and inflection under the different circumstances. The essay cites many idiosyncrasies that would be used in talking with friends, and explains how pronouncing such phrases as "whazup" imply a certain amount of casualness and informality. The essay contrasts this by saying that it would be proper to use common pronunciation and inflection during a job interview, and provides examples of such pronunciation and inflection, as well as describing why it would be employed.

The final paragraph of this essay returns to its central thesis, clearly stating the reasons why one would use language in different ways in different circumstances, casual and informal when talking with friends to reflect a laid-back attitude, but formal and conventional during a job interview to express intelligence and respect.

SAMPLE ESSAY: Satisfactory

When I talk with a friend, I use a different language than I do at a job interview. There are differences in the two, which are reflected in the way I speak. When I talk to a friend, I would be informal and not concerned with showing off my vocabulary or using correct grammar, and I would be inclined to use slang.

When I'm with friends, my pronunciation and inflection reflect the common ways we speak—casual and cool. At a job interview, I would speak in a formal manner to show my potential employer I am mature and have a firm grasp of the English language.

With a friend, I would be more likely to use phrases from popular culture. I might say "That's cool" or make a reference to something on MTV instead of saying "I like that" or "I am fond of that." I would never use that language during a job interview. I would speak clearly to show my potential employer I can speak intelligently. If a potential employer asks me what I think of school, I would not say "It's cool" or "It sucks." I would think a few minutes and say, " I like Macbeth, but I find chemistry challenging."

I may use one syllable words, word that have not meaning, or grammatically incorrect English when I am with a friend. At a job interview, I would not address a potential employer like a peer. I would speak in an even tone, "Hello, It's nice to meet you." I would follow the statement with, "How are you?" My voice would rise to show I am very interested in what the person is doing. This would continue throughout the interview. I would make sure I used my vocabulary in an intelligent way, and I used proper grammar. This will show my potential employer I am respectful and smart.

My use of language with my friends is like my relationships — casual, informal, and idiosyncratic. Conversely, during a job interview, I would speak properly and formally to make a positive impression on the interviewer. I would demonstrate to the interviewer that I am an intelligent human being who is capable of communicating clearly and effectively with all people.

ANALYSIS

As this is a comparison essay, it involves a discussion of the differences and similarities between two concepts. The introduction names the two concepts that will be contrasted, and contains a thesis statement which tells how the concepts differ, in this case providing an overview of the differences between talking with a friend and talking with a potential employer. The writing in the introduction is stylistically sloppy. The sentences are short and somewhat unclear. Only one of the items being compared—talking to a friend—is explained, whereas the language used at a job interview is not discussed at all.

In the body of the essay, the writer first discusses the differences in pronunciation and inflection when speaking with a friend or to a job interviewer, but does not support his or her views with concrete examples. Next, the writer discusses the differences in phrasing in these two different situations. This paragraph is better developed as it has concrete examples to support the essay writer's views. In the following paragraph, the writer provides an example of the language used while addressing a potential employer, but not that used while addressing a friend.

For the most part, this essay is well organized and thorough. It lacks proper development and concrete examples from the text, and at times the writing is sloppy or unclear, but with some revision, this could be a good essay.

SAMPLE ESSAY: Unsatisfactory

The language I use with a friend is different from the language I use during a job interview. My purposes would be different in each case. With a freind. I would be informal and not concerned with showing off my vocabulary or using correct grammar. I would be more inclined to use slang.

My pronunciation and inflection would reflect the common ways, my friends and I speak—casual and cool.

In talking with a friend, I would use phrase drawn from popular culture. For example, I might say "That's cool" or make a reference to MTV. I know my friends and I use the same language. If a friend asked me about school, I would say "Sometimes it's cool and sometimes it sucks."

In talking with friends, I would use phrases such as "hey," "like," and "you know." The phrases would be unconventional and grammatically incorrect. Upon greeting a friend, I would say, "Hay man, what's up."

In talking with a friend, I would enhance my vocabulary with words that have no meaning. I would say, "He is like" to imply the person whom I was speaking was very drunk.

My use of language with a friend would be casual, cool, and idiosyncratic, which reflects our relationship. At a job interview, I would speak proper and formally. This will make a positive impression on the job interviewer and show him or her that I am intelligent and capable of communicating clearly and effectively with all people.

ANALYSIS

The introductory paragraph contains the essay's thesis statement "The language I use with a friend is different from the language I use during a job interview." The writer reinforces this point by stressing the different purposes of language in sentence two. The paragraph is weakened by a fragment ("With a friend") and a spelling error ("freind" should be "friend").

The second paragraph, merely a sentence long, is far too short to adequately develop the idea that is introduced. The writer discusses the pronunciation and inflection used when talking with a friend but provides no information about the pronunciation and inflection used at a job interview. In addition, the essay writer provides no concrete examples to support each point. In paragraph three the writer discusses the phrasing one uses with a friend, but once again does not provide parallel information by giving an example of the phrasing used at a job interview. The following paragraph, in which phrasing is discussed again, should have been combined with this paragraph. In the last paragraph of the body of the essay, the writer discusses the way one would enhance vocabulary with a friend, but provides no information or examples of vocabulary used at a job interview.

The final paragraph of this passage does not function effectively as a conclusion. It merely restates information presented earlier in the essay. Furthermore, it contains an error in parallel sentence structure: "proper and formally" should read "properly and formally."

This essay is mediocre in terms of both style and content. Structurally, the essay is not balanced. The essay writer does not discuss language used at a job interview in the body nor provide supporting examples. Grammatically, the essay is weakened by sentence fragments, spelling errors, and errors in parallel structure.

6.3   Sentence Style

Too often, writers in college do not offer the reader an interesting and coherent flow among their sentences. Students often use the same sentence style repeatedly, making the writing sound disjointed, pedestrian, and choppy. Consider the passage that follows:

> "This outline is merely a tool of analysis. It is in the form of questions. It should remind its user of responsibility. It should remind the user that only he or she can provide the answers. We hope we can talk to one another about literature. We hope we can exchange information about it. A given work of fiction should mean something to us. A work of fiction

should be felt completely. We must wrestle with the work.
We must not use others as guides or informants."

Notice how choppy and unrelated the ideas seem. Notice how all the sentences have the form [subject] + [predicate], producing a monotonous tone and halting reading.

Now consider how the original writer, Robert W. Lewis, Jr., in his article from *College English,* actually wrote it:

"This outline is merely a tool of analysis, and being put in the form of questions, it should constantly remind its user that only he or she can provide the answers. We hope we can talk to one another about literature and exchange informed and reasoned opinions about it, but if a given work of fiction is to mean anything to us, if we are to feel and know it completely, we must at one stage wrestle with the work bare-handed, without others as guides or informants."

This version has drive and energy, not just because the words are slightly different, but because it uses sentences of different types and different lengths to convey Mr. Lewis's thoughts and opinions. Notice how Mr. Lewis uses the "if" to lead a clause or phrase to build up energy in the middle of his statement, leading to the emphatic, "we must ... " clause, which "pushes" on to the end. *Sentence variety,* then, or *varying the kinds and lengths of sentences to reflect the emphasis and the flow of your ideas,* is a quality to bring into your personal writing style.

In English, there are several basic ways to write sentences other than by just having a series of simple sentences with a subject and verb pattern. Writers may combine sentences in English to show relationships among ideas in time or in logic. Writers must be careful to show the relationship of one idea to another with the correct combining word or phrase. Below are three short and choppy sentences that illustrate this point:

Peter is the boss. He controls the office. He is very tyrannical.

But a writer *could* combine these three sentences to make one complex sentence (an independent and a dependent clause) in the following way:

> Peter is a tyrannical boss who controls the office.

Not only does the sentence get clearer and more interesting, but it becomes shorter. The sentences don't always get shorter when this is done, but the relationships among ideas do get clearer for the reader when a writer varies sentences effectively.

Writers may, however, *coordinate ideas* to show that ideas have equal value. Writers may combine sentences by using coordinating conjunctions such as *and, but, nor, for, or, yet,* and *so* as logic demands. For example:

> Peter, the boss, controls the office, **and** he is tyrannical.

Writers may *subordinate ideas* to show the logical or temporal (timely) dependence of one idea upon another. In these cases writers use *since, although, because, even though, while, when,* and *if* to show clear relationships between **cause** and **effect, time,** or **conditional dependence.** For example:

> **Since** Peter is the boss in charge of the office, he is sometimes tyrannical. [cause...effect]

In the following example, notice how the connecting word **"although"** supports a *different* relationship among the ideas, suggesting contradiction:

> **Although** Peter is the boss, he often acts more like a clerk. [conditional dependence]

Here is an example of a temporal relationship:

> **When** Peter became the boss in charge of the office, he started to act like a tyrant.

Writers may show the relationship among ideas by using **transitions** such as *however, consequently, therefore,* or *thus.*

> Peter is the boss in charge of the office; **consequently,** he is very careful.

> Peter is the boss in charge of the office; **however,** he often acts like a clerk.

Notice how the different relationships among the sentences and their clauses generate different thoughtful responses and considerations for the reader even though the basic message, "Peter is the boss in the office," remains mostly the same.

6.4 Narrative Stance: "I" vs. "It," "He," "She," or "They"

In writing effective essays, a writer must decide upon a *narrative stance,* or *point of view.* If an essay is personal and reflects personal memories, opinions, and ideas, then writing from the point of view of "I" or "we" may be appropriate. But in trying to keep the reader's focus on the subject at hand, and not the writer, it may be best to take the *third person point of view.* As mentioned above in a different context in Chapter 2, it may be preferable to talk not about "I" so much as "it" or "they," keeping the subject at a distance from a personal point of view, while focusing instead on the topic at hand.

6.5 Numbers

As a matter of style, the writer should use numbers in text in a few standard ways, depending upon whether following scientific, A.P.A., or M.L.A. guidelines. The writer must do as instructed by a professor, but use personal judgment otherwise and be consistent. As a final note, it is not considered good writing style to begin a sentence with a number written as a figure as in this sentence:

> "42 people came to the meeting."

The difference between *cardinal* and *ordinal* numbers is also important to know. A cardinal number is simply the number itself or the number of anything: 1, 15, 400, 2368, and so on. An ordinal number is one that places the item or items referred to in a sequence: *first, second, third, fourth,* and so on. Spell out all ordinal numbers that can be expressed in one or two words. A hyphenated ordinal number counts as one word: *twenty-second, thirty-fifth.* For particular rules governing fractions, lists, and other special uses of numbers, consult your handbook.

Problem Solving Example:

Write the following numbers as they would be expressed in formal writing:

1. We expected 329 members to attend the 3rd annual convention.

2. During the past 10 years, we have moved 22 times. We are now living at 225 Maple Street.

3. She won $2,000,000 as the 1st prize winner of the lottery.

4. Please reread page 183 of your textbook; it summarizes all of Chapter 19.

5. The revolutions of the 1840s were a turning point in 19th-century European history.

6. They recently rented an apartment at 39 West 193rd Street.

7. The used to live at 1 5th Avenue.

8. 1,139 protestors attended the rally in Central Park even though the temperature reached 93°.

9. It was estimated that eighteen and one half percent of the population went abroad last year.

10. 1991 was a good year for the newspaper. Even though we printed our issues on nine-inch by fourteen-and-one-half-inch paper, we sold a record number of copies.

1. We expected 329 members to attend the third annual convention.

2. During the past ten years, we have moved twenty-two times. We are now living at 225 Maple Street.

3. She won $2 million as the first prize lottery winner.

4. Please reread page 183 of your textbook; it summarizes all of Chapter 19.

5. The revolutions of the 1840s were a turning point in nineteenth-century European history.

6. They recently rented an apartment at 39 West 193rd Street.

7. The used to live at One Fifth Avenue.

8. One thousand one hundred thirty-nine protestors attended the rally in Central Park even though the temperature reached ninety-three degrees.

9. It was estimated that 18 1/2 percent of the population went abroad last year.

10. Nineteen ninety-one was a good year for the newspaper. Even though we printed our issues on 9-inch by 14 1/2 inch paper, we sold a record number of copies.

6.6 Punctuation

Incorrect punctuation can lead to difficulties and distractions. Consider how punctuation alters the way we read the following sentence:

Woman without her man is lost.

Compare with,

Woman: without her, man is lost.

These two sentences mean the opposite of one another, depending upon how they are punctuated; the words don't change at all. *Careful attention to correct punctuation at the end of the writing process is essential to clear and excellent work.* While every little rule that governs punctuation in English can't be covered in this book, the most common errors with commas and semicolons can be pointed out.

1. Commas are used in conventional ways:

    When addressing someone directly in a sentence:

    > Well, John, shall we go to the store?

    When leading a letter with an informal salutation:

    > Dear John,

    When listing items in series:

    > > We had four books for the trip: a novel, a history, an atlas, and an encyclopedia.

    Some people learned that they may leave out the last comma before the "and" in a series. This is true as long as leaving it out doesn't cause confusion or distract the reader from the intended meaning.

2. Use a comma to separate introductory words, phrases, or clauses in a sentence from the independent clause of the sentence.

    Introductory word:

    > *However,* I could only walk to the library.

    Introductory phrase:

    > *After the meeting,* I could only walk to the library.

Introductory clause:

> *Since the bookstore was closed,* I could only walk to the library.

3. Use commas to set off enclosed words, phrases, or clauses from the main clause of the sentence:

Enclosed word:

> John Smith, *however,* is very smart.

Enclosed phrase:

> John Smith, *a daring young man,* is very smart.

Enclosed clause:

> John Smith, *who is a daring young man,* is very smart.

In each of these cases, the writer could remove the enclosed word, phrase, or clause without changing the meaning of the basic sentence at all. These enclosed items merely add incidental information to the main clause: John Smith is very smart. But if the information offered in a phrase or clause is *essential to the understanding of the subject or other noun,* then *a pair of commas is not needed.* Note the following sentence:

(1)   The files *that are in the main office* are out of date.

(2)   Each *of the students* needs to study English.

If the italicized clause from sentence (1) is removed, someone looking for the right files may get lost or confused or throw out all the files that this company owns. The **relative clause** in *italics, "that are in the main office,"* is *essential* to the identity of the particular files in question, especially if there are several offices in this company. Similarly, if the *italicized phrase* is removed from sentence (2), it is difficult to tell which "each" the writer is talking about.

To punctuate two or more independent clauses (units of language containing a subject and verb that can stand on their own as complete thoughts), there are only three choices:

(1) **[.]** or its equivalent **[?]** or **[!]**

Thus (where IC stands for independent clause):

IC [.] IC.

(2) **[;]**

John is smart, and he is a daring young man.

IC [;] IC. or

IC [;] [conjunctive adverb], IC.

John is smart; he is a daring young man.

John is smart; in addition, he is a daring young man.

(3) **[, and]** or another *coordinating conjunction (for, and, nor, but, or, yet,* and *so)*

John is smart. He is a daring young man.

IC [, and] IC.

The semicolon is perhaps the most troublesome form of punctuation for students when, in fact, its use is very simple. As noted above, the semicolon may be used to join together two or more independent clauses. One other important way in which the semicolon is used is to set off items as units in a series in which the items within each unit have punctuation internal to the unit. Thus:

Three of the world's leaders met at Yalta: Franklin Delano Roosevelt, President of the United States; Winston Churchill, Prime Minister of England; and Joseph Stalin, Premier of the Soviet Union.

So make sure that during editing, punctuation is controlled so as not to confuse, distract, or otherwise "turn off" the audience or reader.

Using the colon [:] in writing is actually fairly simple as well. The rules for mathematics are different from writing. But the colon should be used to introduce a vertical list, to introduce a linear list, or to show equivalence between what is to the left of a colon and what is to the right.

To introduce a linear rather than a vertical list:

The breakfast menu had three items: eggs, cereal, and coffee.

To show equivalence:

Only one thing can save us now: robotics.

Any kind of syntactical string can follow a colon: a word, a series of words, a phrase or a series of parallel phrases, a clause or a series of parallel phrases, a sentence or a series of sentences parallel in structure.

Parentheses [(_ _ _ _ _ _)] are used the way a pair of commas is used—to enclose added but inessential information to the syntax of a sentence. A pair of parentheses may be used instead of a pair of commas, but the information placed in the parentheses will not be regarded as important as that placed between a pair of commas. Remember that readers have a tendency to read past material that is in parentheses. Remember also that parentheses should always be used in pairs (some writers forget to close their parenthetical remarks).

Dashes [—] may be used in the place of any other form of punctuation. Most, often, however, they are used in pairs to show a sudden interruption of thought within a sentence. Again, always use them in pairs when you use them this way:

John Smith—what a thinker—is certain to get the job.

Be careful not to use dashes too frequently. Many consider dashes informal and their use tends to make writing seem rushed and disorganized. Dashes are effective when used sparingly—anything can be overdone. Remember that a dash on a computer should be expressed as an em-dash (—), and on a typewriter it should be expressed as two hyphens (--), not one (-).

For special cases of quotation marks with question marks, exclamation points, and other quotation marks, consult a grammar handbook. With respect to the comma, the period, the semicolon, and the colon, certain specific rules for end, or closing quotation marks apply.

Always leave the end quotation mark for a word, phrase, clause, or whole sentence outside a period or a comma. Thus:

Mr. Jones thought the building was "outrageously gaudy."

Again:

Even though Mr. Jones thought the building was "outrageously gaudy," he avowed that the architect had talent.

In the case of a semicolon or colon, however, *always leave the end or closing quotation mark inside the colon or semicolon in question.* Thus:

Mr. Jones thought the building was "outrageously gaudy"; however, he avowed that the architect had talent.

or again:

Mr. Jones thought the building was "outrageously gaudy"— too imitative, too derivative, and too "adolescent" in its style.

Problem Solving Example:

Q All of the needed punctuation and other aspects of mechanics have been omitted from the following passage. There may often be more than one way of correcting the error. Therefore, try taking into account the mood and tone of the writing and the overall coherence of the piece when punctuating the passage.

my sister amy had finally finished packing for college at about 11 am what a day it was as usual she had overpacked but this is an understatement standing in the hallway were the following seven large blue suitcases three borrowed trunks four old bulging macys shopping bags and two duffel bags but im going halfway across the united states how many times do you think ill be coming home she asked once every five years at christmastime i guessed i do hope youll write she said seriously do you know the difference between the words pack and hoard i asked amy laughed self consciously civilization does exist in chicago illinois i added trust me it really does really remarked amy with her own personal brand of sarcasm after all its only the 1990s its well known that three fourths of chicago is still unsettled territory i turned away in disgust it was useless

i went. to help amy with her baggage picking up the large overstuffed green duffel bag i screamed whats in here is this a 50 or 100 pound bag you have got to be kidding i added she had filled the entire bag with books and magazines i knew shed want to take a few of her favorites the stranger by albert camus great expectations by charles dickens king lear by william shakespeare copies of keats and t s eliots best poems and some copies of national geographic but i realized i was all wrong instead she had packed thirty copies of tolstoys war and peace or so it seemed one lone copy of websters new collegiate dictionary remained on her bookshelf in fact it was an extra one she had received for her birthday last year i believe the rest of the move was sadly repetitious i realized amy was nuts

i wasnt about to reason with her i was tired it was futile and there was no time meanwhile amy was totally calm and relaxed as she went through the radio stations she finally settled on one and she listened to the beatles hey jude i seemingly all powerful carried the last trunk out the door the plane a *747 was* scheduled to leave at 12 oclock we were 10 minutes off schedule when we arrived at kennedy airport furthermore i had to pay a $5.00 surcharge for the extra baggage amy said she had only large bills as she was about to board the plane after 101 good byes i handed her a package as if she really needed anything else its a green pullover sweater just like mine i said tearfully oh you really shouldn't have please take it back amy replied theres no time for humility your plane is about to take offi said really you should keep it yours is. already on the plane along with a few other things it took me a few moments to realize what she meant then i said one last final good bye to amy my ex sister.

A   CORRECTED PASSAGE

My sister, Amy, had finally finished packing for college at about 11 a.m. What a day it was! As usual, she had overpacked—but this is an understatement. Standing in the hallway were the following: seven large, blue suitcases; three borrowed trunks; four old, bulging Macy's shopping bags; and two duffel bags.

"But I'm going halfway across the United States! How many times do you think I'll be coming home?" she asked.

"Once every five years at Christmas time?" I guessed.

"I do hope you'll write," she said.

"Seriously, do you know the difference between the words 'pack' and 'hoard'?" I asked. Amy laughed self-consciously.

"Civilization does exist in Chicago, Illinois," I added. "Trust me; it really does."

"Really?" remarked Amy, with her own personal brand of sarcasm. "After all, it's only the 1990s: It's well-known that three-fourths of Chicago is still unsettled territory."

I turned away in disgust. It was useless.

I went to help Amy with her baggage. Picking up the large, overstuffed green duffel bag, I screamed, "What's in here! Is this a fifty- or a hundred-pound bag?" "You have got to be kidding," I added.

She had filled the entire bag with books and magazines. I knew she'd want to take a few of her favorites—*The Stranger,* by Albert Camus; *Great Expectations,* by Charles Dickens; *King Lear,* by William Shakespeare; copies of Keats's and T.S. Eliot's best poems; and some copies of *National Geographic*—but I realized I was all wrong; instead, she had packed thirty copies of Tolstoy's *War and Peace,* or so it seemed. One lone copy of *Webster's New Collegiate Dictionary* remained on her bookshelf; in fact, it was an extra one she had received for her birthday last year. I believe the rest of the move was sadly repetitious. I realized Amy was nuts.

I wasn't about to reason with her: I was tired, it was futile, and there was no time. Meanwhile, Amy was totally calm and relaxed as she went through the radio stations. She finally settled on one, and she listened to the Beatles' "Hey Jude." I, seemingly all-powerful, carried the last trunk out the door.

The plane, a *747,* was scheduled to leave at 12 o'clock. We were ten minutes off schedule when we arrived at Kennedy airport; furthermore, I had to pay a five-dollar surcharge for the extra baggage: Amy said she had only large bills. As she was about to board the plane (after 101 good-byes), I handed her a package—as if she really needed anything else! "It's a green pullover sweater just like mine," I said tearfully. "Oh, you really shouldn't have. Please take it back," Amy replied. "There's no time for humility: your plane is about to take off," I said.

"Really, you should keep it! Yours is already on the plane—along with a few other things."

It took me a few moments to realize what she meant; then, I said one last, final good-bye to Amy, my ex-sister.

Quiz: Some Basics About Good Style

DIRECTIONS: For each sentence in which you find an error, select the one underlined part that must be changed to make the sentence correct and circle the answer.

1. In 1877 Chief Joseph of the Nez Percés, <u>together with</u> 250 warriors
                                          A

    and 500 women and children, <u>were praised</u> by newspaper reporters
                                      B

    for <u>bravery</u> during the 115-day fight <u>for</u> freedom. <u>No error.</u>
         C   **D**   **E**

    A.   B.   C.   D.   E.

2. The ideals <u>upon which</u> American society <u>is based</u> <u>are</u> primarily
                A   **B**   **C**

    those of Europe, and not ones <u>derived from</u> the native Indian cul-
                                    D

    ture. <u>No error.</u>
         E

    A.   B.   C.   D.   E.

3. <u>An astute and powerful</u> woman, Frances Nadel <u>was</u> a beauty
             A   **B**

    contest winner before she <u>became</u> president of the company
                           C

    <u>upon the death</u> of her husband. <u>No error.</u>
         D   **E**

    A.   B.   C.   D.   E.

4. Representative Wilson <u>pointed out</u>, however, that the legislature
                           A

had not finalized the state budget and salary increases had de-
      B   **C**

pended on decisions to be made in a special session. No error.
                                D   **E**

   A.   B.   C.   D.   E.

5.   Now the city librarian, doing more than checking out books, must
              A

help to plan puppet shows and movies for children, garage sales
      B

for used books, and arranging for guest lectures and exhibits for
    C   **D**

adults. No error.
      E

   A.   B.   C.   D.   E.

DIRECTIONS: In each of the following sentences, some part or all of the sentence is underlined. Below each sentence you will find five ways of phrasing the underlined part. Select the answer that produces the most effective sentence, one that is clear and exact, without awkwardness or ambiguity. In choosing your answers, follow the requirements of standard written English. Choose the answer that best expresses the meaning of the original sentence. Answer (A) is always the same as the underlined part. Choose it if you think the original sentence needs no revision.

6.   Being that you bring home more money than I do, it is only fitting you should pay proportionately more rent.

     (A)   Being that you bring home more money than I do

     (B)   Bringing home the more money of the two of us

     (C)   When more money is made by you than me

     (D)   Because you bring home more money than I do

     (E)   If you're bringing home more money than me

7. So tenacious is their grip on life, that sponge cells will regroup and form a new sponge even <u>when they are squeezed</u> through silk.

   (A) when they are squeezed

   (B) since they have been

   (C) as they will be

   (D) after they have been

   (E) because they should be

8. <u>Seeing as how the plane is late</u>, wouldn't you prefer to wait for a while on the observation deck?

   (A) Seeing as how the plane is late

   (B) When the plane come is

   (C) Since the plane is late

   (D) Being as the plane is late

   (E) While the plane is landing

9. Only with careful environmental planning can we protect the <u>world we live in.</u>

   (A) world we live in.

   (B) world in which we live in.

   (C) living in this world.

   (D) world's living.

   (E) world in which we live.

10. In the last three years, we have added more varieties of vegetables to our garden <u>than those you suggested in the beginning.</u>

    (A)   than those you suggested in the beginning.

    (B)   than the ones we began with.

    (C)   beginning with your suggestion.

    (D)   than what you suggested to us.

    (E)   which you suggested in the beginning.

ANSWER KEY

1.	(E)	6.	(D)
2.	(C)	7.	(C)
3.	(D)	8.	(A)
4.	(D)	9.	(D)
5.	(A)	10.	(E)

CHAPTER 7

Handling Research Assignments

7.1 Planning Time

During the course of a college career, you will write research papers, sometimes in a technical field, and sometimes about literature itself. Whatever the assignment is, the purpose of research papers is to develop skills in finding out information, evaluating what was found, and giving the reader either new information or a new insight into information already known. Research papers are generally longer than the average 500-word essay required in most composition courses, so plan more carefully for them. They vary in length from 3,000 to 5,000 words on average. In this section, we will discuss the special needs of the research paper.

Writing a research paper is a long-term project; consequently, time must be scheduled during a term so that the completed paper can be delivered on time. Since the research paper must go through the same stages as any essay, use the stages of the writing process to plan time. Whatever time you have, a paper should be scheduled in such a manner that it can be completed by your professor's deadline.

Your research paper is basically another paper that must be written using the writing process. During the *prewriting stage,* use the time to gather research materials at the library. Do not hesitate to seek the help of a *research librarian in the library at your college*. Research librarians can point out where to find the information sources the writer needs.

Basically, a student may find research material in either a *card catalog* or an *automated catalog*. Most libraries now have automated catalogs, so it is helpful to learn to use them effectively. Typical screens from automated catalogs are show in Figures 1-4.

---

261 Alexander Library   —IRIS Library System - All * Choose Search

What type of search do you wish to do?

     1. TIL   – Title, journal title, series title, etc.

     2. AUT – Author, illustrator, editor, organization, etc.

     3. SUB – Subject heading assigned by library.

     4. NUM – Call number, ISBN, ISSN, etc.

     5. BOL – Boolean/Keyword search on title, author, and subject.

     6. LIM – Limit your search to a portion of the catalog.

Enter number or code, then press enter <CR>; to exit type END.

Figure 1: *An example of a main menu from an automated catalog.*

---

261 Alexander Library   —IRIS Library System - All * Choose Search

    Start at the beginning of the title and enter as many
    words of the title as you know below

        EX: Wuthering Heights

        EX: How to Succeed in Business Without

Enter title: Then press SEND

Figure 2: *An example of the menu for an automated catalog search by title.*

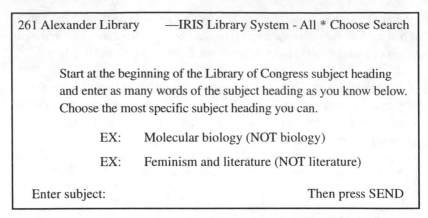

261 Alexander Library —IRIS Library System - All * Choose Search

Start at the beginning of the Library of Congress subject heading and enter as many words of the subject heading as you know below. Choose the most specific subject heading you can.

EX: Molecular biology (NOT biology)

EX: Feminism and literature (NOT literature)

Enter subject: Then press SEND

Figure 3: An example of the menu for an automated catalog search by subject.

261 Alexander Library —IRIS Library System - All * Choose Search

Enter last name first.

EX: Bronte, Emily

EX: Mondarin, Piet

Enter author: Then press SEND

Figure 4: An example of the menu for an automated catalog search by author.

Sources that should be sought out in the library include, of course, books *relevant to the topic that can be found in the Library of Congress subject headings* or, in some libraries, in the *Dewey Decimal System.* These are the systems used to catalog information in most libraries. The writer must learn to use the systems to find what he or she needs.

In addition to books, the writer may use *periodicals* and *journals* that are relevant to the topic. The *Reader's Guide to Periodical Literature* and *New York Times Index* are the two best sources for this information.

Indexes for special disciplines such as psychology or medicine are available. Finally, various *abstracting services* are available to provide summaries of important recent articles and books relevant to a project.

In addition to books, periodicals, and journals, students can now use the Internet. The Internet provides information via the World Wide Web on any subject, such as Thomas Wolfe. To access this, the student types in the name of the subject he or she wishes to research in the field provided and presses "search." Then, listings of web pages appear. A sample listing is shown below.

> **The Thomas Wolfe Web Site**
> URL: http://www/cms/uncwil.edu/~connelly/wolfe/html

Below each listing is a summary of the information contained in the web site. The student should read the summary, and then decide if he or she wishes to view the web site. If the student chooses to view the web site, then he or she clicks on the web site name or the URL, and the web page appears.

An Internet resource must be documented. Below is the format for documenting an Internet resource.

> Author. Title of item. [Online] Available
> http://address/file name, date or document or download.

A sample documentation is shown below.

> Connelly, Sharon S. The Thomas Wolfe Web Page [Online]
> Available
> http.//www.cms.uncwil.edu/connelly/wolfe.html, June 19, 1997.

Additional information on citing electronic sources can be found by accessing the MLA Citation Guide at the web address below.

> MLA Citation Guide
> URL: http://www.cas.usf.edu/english/walker/mla/html.

After having discovered how to use these resources, the writer should develop a *working bibliography,* that is, *a list on index cards of all the sources that **might** be used in the paper.* The writer must be sure to include all the *bibliographic information* on one side of the cards (including *author, title, publisher, city of publication, year of publication,* and *any other identifying information necessary*). Put important notes on the other side of the cards, such as the author's thesis or main supporting evidence. The writer should do this in the beginning; these notes will then be available when writing the formal bibliography at the end.

When at the end of the research effort during prewriting, the writer should write a *working outline* of the paper that shows what should be included in the sections of the paper (introduction, body, and conclusion). Use this outline as a rough idea of how and what should be included in the paper. Later, when revising the paper, data may be added as well as ideas that will affect the length and shape of the paper.

Problem Solving Example:

Q Your American Literature professor has asked you to write a research paper about an author you are studying. During your research in the library, you discover F. Scott Fitzgerald and Thomas Wolfe, two of the writers you are studying in class, were acquaintances. You locate a biography of Fitzgerald and his wife that contains information on the two writers' encounters. You jot this information on an index card for your working bibliography. Using the information on your index card, answer the following questions. **Note:** If you do not have an index card, use the space provided below.

Mellow, James R. Invented Lives: F. Scott and Zelda Fitzgerald. Boston: Houghton Mifflin Company, 1984.

   a.   What is the title of the book?

   b.   Name the famous writer who is the subject of the book.

   c.   Who wrote the book?

   d.   Name the publisher of the book?

   e.   What year was the book published?

   f.   Name the city where the book was published?

A

   a.   The title of the book is *Invented Lives: F. Scott and Zelda Fitzgerald.*

   b.   The book is about the famous writer, F. Scott Fitzgerald, and his wife.

   c.   The author of the book is James R. Mellow.

   d.   The publisher is Houghton Mifflin Company.

   e.   The year of publication is 1984.

   f.   The city of publication is Boston.

7.2   Original vs. Derivative Research

Professors may ask for either *original* or *derivative research* or both, depending upon the topic. The opportunity to do *original research* rarely occurs to undergraduates, but this kind of research is characterized by finding out entirely new things in new areas of experiment or study. Most often, graduate students find themselves involved in this sort of research. *Derivative research* is characterized by study and research from works already known and written by experts in a given field, from which the student researcher forms new opinions or from which information is used to support theses *derived from someone else's findings.*

Sometimes professors call upon students to write a *review of the literature* available in a given field. In this sort of research paper, the student is asked to find out what is generally known about a given topic and "review" the literature for its major findings or theses of the experts in the field. In sociology, a student may write a paper about what is known about urban violence among teenagers in Philadelphia. Who are the authorities and what are their theories? Once a working bibliography is developed in addition to a rough outline, the rough draft can be started.

7.3 Primary and Secondary Sources

Before launching into the draft the writer must make sure that both types of sources have been researched: *primary* and *secondary resources*. Some topics do not have primary resources. Make sure that they are being dealt with if both exist. A *primary resource* is the original book, work of art, or artifact under study. For example, *Huckleberry Finn* is the primary resource for the study of the novel *Huckleberry Finn*. Anything written, spoken, or recorded about the primary source that is in the public domain is a *secondary source*. Some sources are better than others. While it may be interesting enough in its own right, Joe the plumber's view of the literary value of *Huckleberry Finn* is probably not as relevant as the view of an expert who has made his or her life study the life and work of Mark Twain. The value of secondary sources can be checked by asking the reference librarian and the professor who assigned the paper.

Problem Solving Example:

Q You have made numerous trips to the library and have discovered many sources in the card catalog, automated card catalog, and electronic data banks, such as Newsbank, Infotrac, and the Internet, which you could use in your working bibliography for your research paper on the relationship between F. Scott Fitzgerald and Thomas Wolfe. Your American Literature professor has asked you to identify each source as being a primary resource (PR) or secondary resource (SR).

_____a. Mellow, James R. *Invented Lives: F. Scott and Zelda Fitzgerald.* Boston:Houghton Mifflin, 1984.

_____b. Wolfe, Thomas, *The Web and the Rock.* New York: Harper and Row, 1937.

_____c. Turnbull, Andrew, ed. *The Letters of F. Scott Fitzgerald.* New York: Charles Scribner's, 1963.

_____d. LeVot, Andre. "Fitzgerald in Paris," FHA (1973) 49-68.

_____e. Berg, A. Scott. *Max Perkins: Editor of Genius.* New York: Pocket Books, 1979.

_____f. Austin, Neal F. *A Biography of Thomas Wolfe.* Austin, Texas: Robert Beacham, 1968.

_____g. Fitzgerald, F. Scott. *This Side of Paradise.* New York: Charles Scribner's Sons, 1920.

_____h. Turnbull, Andrew. *Thomas Wolfe.* New York: Charles Scribner's Sons, 1967.

A

a. *Invented Lives* is a secondary resource.

b. *The Web and the Rock* is a primary resource.

c. *The Letters of F. Scott Fitzgerald* is a secondary resource.

d. "Fitzgerald in Paris" is a secondary resource.

e. *Max Perkins: Editor of Genius* is a secondary resource.

f. *A Biography of Thomas Wolfe* is a secondary resource.

g. *This Side of Paradise* is a primary resource.

h. *Thomas Wolfe* is a secondary resource.

7.4 Outlining: The Fundamental Form for Research Papers

Research takes slightly different forms depending upon what field the paper is in; however, the basic form of introduction, body, and conclusion remains, and should be followed along with the current form used in the field of study. Get to know the forms particular to the field.

7.4.1 Introduction, Background, Discussion and Analysis, Implications, Conclusions, and Recommendations

Although the basic pattern of organization is the same for research papers as for shorter essays, some differences are important to note.

The *introduction* to a research paper usually includes a statement of the paper's purpose, the topic to be explored, and the fundamental thesis or hypothesis of the writer.

The next section, or *background,* usually discusses the "history," or extant of published knowledge available about the topic, and summarizes the known theories and research. If researching the "causes of violence among urban teenagers in Philadelphia," the *background* section would summarize all the major known causes cited by authorities and independent studies in the field.

Next, the *discussion and analysis* section should offer views of what the known research indicates and how it affects the thesis (Does it support the thesis, contradict it, or do a little of both? Does the research found in favor of the thesis outweigh that opposed?). In this section, the writer should not offer any statements that are conclusive about the thesis, but only explain and analyze the findings that came out of the research.

In the next section, or *implications,* the writer should show what the information researched *implies* about the *thesis,* or say *what the trends are; what the dominant theories are;* and *what makes the most sense.* The writer must be sure to give credit to those scholars or researchers from whose work he has derived ideas, by quoting, paraphrasing, and always citing sources where necessary.

In the *conclusions and recommendations* section, the writer must list the findings and what he or she believes to be the truth about the topic and the power of the thesis. The conclusions should be (1) logically inescapable, given the research; (2) limited in scope appropriate to the level of research; and (3) not the restatement of someone else's ideas. A writer may include *recommendations* to add to the paper. Usually, if offering the solution to a problem, recommendations would be in order. Also, young researchers will often recommend areas of research that other researchers need to pursue further because they have been overlooked, slighted, or neglected because the findings remain inconclusive. Generally, however, in a research paper about literature, the writer will limit his or her conclusion to the meaning or relevance of a work of literary art.

A LIST OF REFERENCE STYLE BOOKS
FOR RESEARCH PAPERS

American Psychological Association. *Publication Manual of the American Psychological Association.* Latest edition. Washington D.C.: American Psychological Association.

Associated Press. *The Associated Press Stylebook and Libel Manual.* Reading: Addison, 1987.

The Chicago Manual of Style. Latest edition. Chicago: University of Chicago Press.

Gibaldi, Joseph, and Walter S. Achtert. *MLA Handbook for Writers of Research Papers.* Latest edition. New York: Modern Language Association.

REA's Handbook of English Grammar, Style and Writing. Latest edition. Piscataway, N. J.: Research and Education Association.

Turabian, Kate L. *A Manual for Writers of Term Papers, Theses, and Dissertations.* Latest edition. Chicago: University of Chicago Press.

United States Government Printing Office. *Style Manual* Rev. ed. Washington D.C.: GPO.

The final *bibliography* is *an alphabetical listing of every book; periodical, abstract, article, dissertation, interview, or any other information that the writer reads while writing the paper, whether using the information in that source or not.* The writer must check the style manual that is correct for the discipline of the paper written. If the researcher only looked at the title of a particular source, or just scanned it, without using any information from that source, the writer does not need to include it in the bibliography.

Problem Solving Examples:

Q Your American Literature professor has asked you to organize your thoughts into an outline. He tells you that an outline is one possible way for a writer to approach his topic. He asks you to identify the introduction, body, and conclusion of your research paper about the relationship between F. Scott Fitzgerald and Thomas Wolfe. Write the appropriate section of the paper (intro, body, etc.) in each space provided.

____ I.   F. Scott Fitzgerald and Thomas Wolfe had a love-hate relationship. The two writers disliked each other, yet felt mutual admiration. Fitzgerald wanted to be as good a writer as Wolfe, while Wolfe desired Fitzgerald's sophistication.

____ II.   Maxwell Perkins, Fitzgerald and Wolfe's editor at Scribners, had arranged for the two writers to meet. Each writer had a different kind of relationship with Perkins. To Fitzgerald, Perkins was always a source of money when the writer had financial difficulties. To Wolfe, Perkins was a father figure.

____ III. The two writers met four times: Europe; Brooklyn; New York City; and Asheville, North Carolina. Each meeting will be detailed.

____ IV.   Four letters were exchanged between the writers. The letters reveal the writers' feelings toward each other.

____ V.   In conclusion, Thomas Wolfe turned his friendship with F. Scott Fitzgerald into jealousy over money and status.

I. Introduction. This will be your research paper's introduction. It will state your thesis that there was animosity between the two writers.

II. Body. This will be the first paragraph of your research paper's body. It is a good first paragraph because it explains how Maxwell Perkins instigated the writers' first meeting. This paragraph will also show the differing views each writer had toward their mutual editor.

III. Body. The second body paragraph builds upon the writers' first meeting by providing details of each meeting that followed. The details include date, place, and a description of the meeting.

IV. Body. The third and final body paragraph focuses on the writers' correspondence. It reveals what the writers said in letters to each other. In this paragraph, the animosity surfaces.

V. Conclusion. This concluding paragraph will summarize the information presented in the body and show the way the writers' relationship changed through the years.

Problem Solving Examples:

Q You have completed the text of your research paper on the relationship between F. Scott Fitzgerald and Thomas Wolfe. Now, it is time to compile your bibliography. Your professor has asked that your sources be listed in alphabetical order. As you look at your index cards, you notice they are NOT in alphabetical order. Place your sources in alphabetical order by writing 1, 2, 3, and 4, etc. in the blank provided.

_____a.   Mellow, James R. *Invented Lives: F. Scott and Zelda Fitzgerald.* Boston: Houghton Mifflin, 1984.

_____b.   Wolfe, Thomas. *The Web and the Rock.* New York: Harper and Row, 1937.

_____c. Turnbull, Andrew, ed. *The Letters of F. Scott Fitzgerald.* New York: Charles Scribner's, 1963.

_____d. LeVot, Andre. "Fitzgerald in Paris," FHA (1973) 49-68.

_____e. Berg, A. Scott. *Max Perkins: Editor of Genius.* New York: Pocket Books, 1979.

_____f. Austin, Neal. *A Biography of Thomas Wolfe.* Austin, Texas: Robert Beacham, 1968.

_____g. Fitzgerald, F. Scott. *This Side of Paradise.* New York: Charles Scribner's, 1920.

_____h. Turnbull, Andrew. *Thomas Wolfe.* New York: Charles Scribner's, 1967.

A

5
_____a. Mellow, James R. *Invented Lives: F. Scott and Zelda Fitzgerald.* Boston: Houghton Mifflin, 1984.

8
_____b. Wolfe, Thomas. *The Web and the Rock.* New York: Harper and Row, 1937.

6
_____c. Turnbull, Andrew, ed. *The Letters of F. Scott Fitzgerald.* New York: Charles Scribner's, 1963.

4
_____d. LeVot, Andre. "Fitzgerald in Paris," FHA (1973) 49-68.

2
_____e. Berg, A. Scott. *Max Perkins: Editor of Genius.* New York: Pocket Books, 1979.

1
_____f. Austin, Neal. *A Biography of Thomas Wolfe.* Austin, Texas: Robert Beacham, 1968.

3
_____g. Fitzgerald, F. Scott. *This Side of Paradise.* New York: Charles Scribner's, 1920.

<u>7</u>   h. Turnbull, Andrew. *Thomas Wolfe.* New York: Charles Scribner's, 1967.

7.4.2 Documentation and Plagiarism

One of the serious problems in writing research papers is that students often have difficulty citing or *documenting correctly the research they have done.* If a researcher uses an idea and the very same words directly from some other writing or research, the researcher must make sure that he or she has correctly noted the sources for the reader. This type of documentation not only helps readers do further research if they want to work with the same information, but it also honors the work of those who previously spent so much time and effort to find out about the chosen topic.

Students and writers who do not note where they got information, or *take another person's ideas and represent them as one's own,* are guilty of *plagiarism.* In most colleges, this is a serious problem sometimes worthy of expelling the student found guilty of it. *The writer must not plagiarize.* It doesn't matter how much the writer borrows from another author as long as he or she acknowledges the ideas which are not original.

To document correctly, a writer must follow specific forms, depending upon the discipline for the writing; e.g., the forms for psychology are slightly different from the forms for English, and so on. One or more of the books listed in 7.4.1 may be bought to use as a guide to the special paper formats, references, and forms of citation and documentation that each discipline includes in the list. Professors prefer to see a variety of primary and secondary resources demonstrating that the student researched a thorough range of possible sources.

7.4.3 Footnotes and Endnotes

In doing research documentation, the researcher may cite where he or she found the information for a particular idea in one of two basic ways: *footnotes* or *endnotes.* Writers generally number *footnotes* sequentially and list them at the bottom of each page in which the information or quotation is footnoted with a line separating the footnote from the text and with a superscript or other number to identify the item referred to within the text.

[1]Jones, R.H., *The Rise of Mammals After the Fall of Dinosaurs.* (New York: Biology Press, 1994) pp. 34-36.

Unlike bibliographies, footnotes and endnotes usually include the particular pages on which the quoted or paraphrased information was found. *Endnotes* are basically the same as footnotes, except that, instead of printing each footnote that appears on a page at the bottom of the page, the researcher places endnotes after the text of the paper, numbering them sequentially on as many pages as needed. The writer usually places endnotes after any *appendices,* sections of information such as charts, graphs, or experimental data, but before the bibliography. The bibliography is always the last section of any paper. Many students dread doing research; however, once they have a full grasp of the techniques, they will find that these techniques have many applications in most professional walks of life. Moreover, the student seldom forgets what he or she researches.

If a writer quotes a piece of information directly from a research source, the writer must footnote the source. If a writer only uses a person's ideas, but not his or her exact words, the writer must footnote that *paraphrase just as if it were a quotation.* A student *may* arrive independently at an idea that some expert in the topic under study has already found, but that rarely happens. Such a convergence of thought is usually a sign of weak research. The student who knows the available sources well enough knows that he or she shared an idea with an expert in the field. To be safe, footnote any idea that is not an original. It is better to footnote too much rather than too little.

Quiz: Handling Research Assignments

1. In a bibliographic entry, the name of the publishing company appears just

   (A) before the city of publication.

   (B) after the city of publication.

   (C) before the publication title.

   (D) after the publication title.

   (E) after the author's name.

2. The most likely source for a brief overview of Mao Zedong's childhood would be

   (A) a magazine article.

   (B) an encyclopedia article.

   (C) a biography.

   (D) a world history book.

   (E) the biographical section of a dictionary.

3. In an encyclopedia article, a cross-reference

   (A) is a type of asterisk.

   (B) gives the titles of books on the same subject.

   (C) explains the difference between the subject discussed and another subject.

   (D) appears at top of each page.

   (E) identifies a related article in the same encyclopedia.

4. When citing a single source in the text of a research paper, the page number is immediately followed by

   (A) a comma.   (D) a slash.

   (B) a period.   (E) a parenthesis.

   (C) a space.

5. In a student's research paper, which of the following does not need to be documented?

   (A) A bar chart from a textbook.

   (B) A paraphrase of an art critic's comment.

   (C) A direct quote from an ancient Greek philosopher.

   (D) A theory developed by the student who wrote the paper.

   (E) A comment recorded during an interview.

6. A book's index is most practical for

   (A) finding a little information on a specific subject.

   (B) locating every illustration in the book.

   (C) identifying subjects related to the book's main topic.

   (D) determining the reading level of the book.

   (E) finding the author's reference sources.

7. The least important information for finding a specific magazine article at the library is

   (A) the name of the magazine.

   (B) the issue number of the magazine.

    (C)   the page numbers of the article.

    (D)   whether the article is illustrated.

    (E)   whether the article is continued in the next issue.

8.   In text citations, an author's name usually appears

    (A)   first name, then last name.

    (B)   last name, then first name.

    (C)   either last name only or last name plus first initial.

    (D)   last name plus first initial in all cases.

    (E)   last name only in all cases.

9.   In a direct quotation, a text citation should appear just after

    (A)   the name of the person quoted.

    (B)   the last word in the quotation.

    (C)   the period or ellipsis at the end of the quotation.

    (D)   the quotation mark ending the quotation.

    (E)   the last word in the paragraph.

10.   When looking for a book in the library, it is least important to remember

    (A)   the catalog call number.

    (B)   the book title.

    (C)   the author's name.

    (D)   the date of publication.

    (E)   whether the book is oversized.

ANSWER KEY

1. (B)
2. (B)
3. (E)
4. (E)
5. (D)

6. (A)
7. (D)
8. (C)
9. (D)
10. (E)

CHAPTER 8

Essay Tests

8.1 Successfully Taking Essay Tests

In college English and other courses, professors usually require students to take essay tests on course material. The students must be ready to take these tests, moving through the questions quickly. Here are some useful steps to follow:

Plan a strategy for the test and study materials from the course. All night cramming for tests is rarely effective. Don't let this happen. Plan ahead. In particular, make sure to allot enough time for writing the essay. To do this, modify the writing process to meet the needs of the test. A student should do most of the prewriting before the test as he or she researches and studies it. Once in the classroom, don't panic. Make a time scheme based on the number of questions and the amount of time allotted for the test.

1. *Read the directions carefully. If possible, read a model set before the test.* This will save valuable time.

2. *Determine a thesis in response to the question.* If there is more than one question, do what appears to be the easiest question first. Decide on the response and thesis and stick to it. Use key words from the question to frame the response. If the question

is, "How does Mark Twain use the river in *Huckleberry Finn?"* a logical response might begin, "Mark Twain uses the river in *Huckleberry Finn* to show ..." In any case, don't be wishy-washy; take a stand in the thesis statement and make a case for it.

3. *Jot down some quick notes about areas that must be included in the response and decide on the order of ideas.* Don't try to make a perfect outline; simply list your major ideas and a few details that are relevant from the course material for the test.

4. *Write a rough draft from these notes quickly and without stopping to check for editing errors in sentence structure, punctuation, and spelling.* The main job during this time is to get ideas onto the paper in order to review and change them quickly in the time allowed. During this time, write on every other line and write on one side of the paper only. The examiner will always have an extra "blue book" (a blank booklet of paper colleges often used for exams) or more paper; so space is not a concern. Don't make an effort to erase every mistake; get all thoughts down on paper first. It is often tempting to write more, but only write what was planned. Take a quick break by looking away from the paper for a minute or two.

5. *Make sure that the form of the essay has been accounted for by checking for correct format, and that an introduction, body, and conclusion was included.* Make sure that paragraphs have been indented correctly; and if a paragraph or two has been added at the end, be sure that the professor knows where they should go. Quickly check the details and transitions to make sure the thesis is supported and the ideas flow by using effective transitions.

6. *Check the editing and proofread quickly.* As the essay is scanned, *make sure that the sentences are complete* and not fragments. Know what kinds of errors are usually made, look for them, and make corrections on the lines in between that were left blank when writing the draft. Eliminate any obvious frivolous or mindless errors, such as writing "bare" for "bear."

Problem Solving Example:

Q Examine the following passage by Edgar Allan Poe. Then write an essay that defines and discusses the effect of the selection on the reader. Pay particular attention to how the writer uses syntax, diction, imagery, tone, and argument to produce that effect.

For the most wild yet most homely narrative which I am about to pen, I neither expect nor solicit belief. Mad indeed would I be to expect it, in a case where my very senses reject their own evidence. Yet, mad am I not—and very surely do I not dream. But tomorrow I die, and today I would unburden my soul. My immediate purpose is to place before the world, plainly, succinctly, and without comment, a series of mere household events. In their consequences, these events have terrified—have tortured—have destroyed me. Yet I will not attempt to expound them. To me, they have presented little but horror—to many they will seem less terrible than baroque. Hereafter, perhaps, some intellect may be found which will reduce my phantasm to the commonplace—some intellect more calm, more logical, and far less excitable than my own, which will perceive, in the circumstances I detail with awe, nothing more than an ordinary succession of very natural causes and effects.

A This Answer provides sample essays which represent possible responses to the essay topic. Compare your own response to those given on the next few pages. Allow the strengths and weaknesses of the sample essays to help you critique your own essay and improve your writing skills.

SAMPLE ESSAY: Well-written

The main effect of this passage is to foster in readers an anticipation of the horror that will be found in what otherwise might be considered "everyday" events which will be described in the following pages.

It is fitting that the author chooses to create this tone of fearful anticipation by juxtaposing the promise of extraordinary emotional impact with the images and reality of seemingly ordinary descriptions ("household events"). In the first line, the author portrays a dichtomy in the phrase, "most wild yet most homely." The passage goes on to directly state that "mere household events" have "terrified—have tortured—have destroyed me." Here he reemphasizes the surprising conversion of the everyday into the extraordinary by saying that these events are horrible to him, yet they may seem little more than frivolous exaggerations *("baroques")* to others. Finally, he states that some day, the extraordinary events he is about to chronicle may be interpreted by others "more logical" as "commonplace"—an oblique reference to possible madness.

Referring to himself as "mad" instead of insane, anticipating that others might think his story will be *"baroque"* instead of simply elaborate, and claiming that what he has experienced might be a "phantasm" instead of a misinterpretation, are intentional word choices designed to create in readers a feeling that they are about to enter a world in which what is real is always open to question—by the author as well as the reader. Others might not see what he has seen, or draw the same conclusions. Poe is, in effect, defining the lines of argument in which he participates ("Mad indeed would I be ... mad I am not") and—he seems to hope—his readers will participate as well.

Repetition and anticipation of the horrible is also seen in Poe's cryptic statement that "tomorrow I die, and today I would unburden my soul." This comment and others in the passage (that he would be mad for the author to think that others will believe him), both motivates readers to continue and indicates to them that they will have to decide whether or not the story's author is mad—whether or not the commonplace events that he will be describing constitute a "phantasm" most extraordinary.

ANALYSIS

The student's response has addressed the main challenge of the question *(an analysis of the effect of the passage on the reader),* and each of its elements: syntax *(the arrangement and interrelationship of words in sentences),* diction *(the use, choice, and arrangement of words in writing),* imagery *(mental images, collectively),* and tone *(defined as a prevailing mood).* The response is delivered with attention to words and phrases from the text and with appropriate interpretations or restatements. The responder also succeeds in defining the central argument Poe implies exists within the writer of the passage, and by extension, the same one he hopes will engage the reader (i.e., is he mad?). The essay itself is delivered in a compact and economic whole in which the conclusion echoes the themes raised in the conclusion. For all these reasons, the essay is quite well-written.

SAMPLE ESSAY: Satisfactory

This passage makes readers anticipate horror in "everyday" events. Poe creates fear by juxtaposing the promise of emotional impact with the image and reality of ordinary description ("household events"). In the first line, the author uses a dichotomy in the phrase "most wild yet most homely." The passage goes on to state "mere household events" have "terrified—have tortured me." Poe goes on to say that these events are horrible to him, but they may have been exaggarated to others. Finally, he states that someday the extraordinary events he is about to chronicle may be logical to others.

Poe refers to himself as "mad" not insane. These are intentional word choices designed to make the readers think they are about to enter a world where real is questionable. Others might not see what he sees or make the same conclusions.

The author's cryptic statement "tomorrow I die and today I would unburden my soul" mirrors the anticipation of horror. Poe wants his readers to continue reading, and he lets them decide weather or not he is mad or the commonplace events he describes are "phantasm."

ANALYSIS

The introduction does not adequately explain the concepts that the essay will explore, and it does not establish the passage that the author is describing. It launches into a brief and unclear sentence that is not sufficiently enticing to make the reader wish to continue with the essay. The paragraph contains one spelling error ("exaggarated" should be spelled "exaggerated").

The body of the essay is much more fully developed than the introduction. Each paragraph is quite well rounded, exploring the topic to a greater extent and supporting it with concrete examples from the text. Unfortunately, some of the sentences are awkwardly constructed to the point that their meaning becomes less clear. Furthermore, although it is good to include examples from the text, it is important to elaborate on them, and to incorporate them into the text in such a way that they support the thesis of the essay. It is confusing to draw a certain conclusion from a part of the text without showing how that conclusion has been reached.

The final paragraph does not quite function as a conclusion. The ideas are not fully developed and the sentences do not function coherently together to form a satisfactory ending for the piece. Although the basic ideas are interesting, they are not stated in such a way that they give the essay closure. The paragraph contains one word choice error ("weather" should be "whether").

For the most part this essay is quite well organized and developed. There are places, however, when, due to a certain awkwardness of phrasing, the writer's statements become unclear. Many of the statements, though important in themselves, are not carefully connected to what comes before and after. The number of mechanical and grammatical errors also detract from the value of this essay. With a little more thought and some revision, this could become quite a good essay.

SAMPLE ESSAY: Unsatisfactory

This passage creates the effect of horror by making readers anticipate it in "everyday" events that seam ordinary.

Poe creates fearful anticipation by juxtaposing the promise of extraordinary emotional impact with images of ordinary descriptions ("household events"). The passage states that household events have terrified him. This is reemphasized in the words "destroyed him." Poe, again, converts the everyday into the extraordinary by saying these events are horrible to him, but they may be exaggerations to others. Finally, Poe says that these events may be interpreted by others as common; thus, meaning, he's mad.

Continuing to refer to himself as "mad," not insane, thinking of what others may say about this, and claiming that he has experienced a "phantasm" instead of misinterpreting an event, are all intentional word choices made by Poe. The choices are designed to influence the readers into thinking they are about to enter a world where reel is questionable.

Poe makes the following questionable statement: "tomorrow I die, and today I would unburden my soul." Poe wants his readers to decide if he is mad.

ANALYSIS

The ideas in this essay are complicated. Poe's passage is quite complex itself, and this particular reading of it contains many subtleties that are difficult to express. Throughout this essay, the writer does not introduce or develop concepts to a sufficient extent to convey the full scope of the ideas he or she introduces. The introduction itself, containing the thesis statement, fails to establish a background for the essay, or to entice the reader to continue reading. The introductory paragraph contains one word choice error ("seam" should be "seems").

When an essay such as this is inadequately introduced, it is difficult for the writer to continue the discussion in the body of the essay without confusing the reader. This is especially true if the concepts presented in the body are insufficiently developed or unsupported, as is the case in this essay. These problems, together with the fact that the writing is choppy and awkward at times, take away from the power of the argument the writer is attempting to make. It would also be helpful for the writer to substantiate his or her thesis with examples from the passage itself. There are quite a few errors in the body of the essay. For instance, "he's" should be "he is," and "reel" should be "real."

Paragraph four, the final paragraph, begins with a quotation "tomorrow I die, and today I would unburden my soul," but the writer fails to explain the significance of these words. The writer also needs to establish a reason for Poe to want his readers to decide if he is mad.

In part because this quotation is unsubstantiated, and in part because the paragraph is brief and unclearly written, it does not bring closure to the essay as a concluding paragraph should.

This essay is not satisfactory because the writer fails to support his or her views with examples and also fails to explain the few quotations from the passage that he or she does include. In addition, the essay contains several spelling and word choice errors, which contribute to the lack of clarity, and which impede the reader's understanding of the difficult concepts tackled in the essay.

The study of college English is the introduction to the control of the international language of trade, business, and scholarship. Without a real grip on how to use English well, a person is already at a loss with respect to the competition. Those who command or control their English in writing are those who usually outshine the competition in any field.

The study of college English is also the introduction to the literary heritage of America, England, and other nations as well as to intellectual and aesthetic benefits that will broaden and deepen the personality and the quality of life.

English is the primary tool by which the world gets its work done. Being without language is like being a carpenter who stands before a plot of land and wants to build the house of his dreams, but has no hammers, no saw, no wood—in short, no tools to get the job done. Thoughts shouldn't stand idle because of an inability to express them thoughtfully and correctly. Develop the tools provided; learn the essentials of college and university writing.

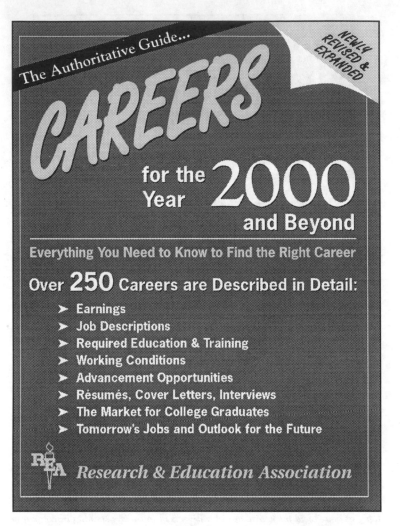

Available at your local bookstore or order directly from us by sending in coupon below.

REA's Test Preps
The Best in Test Preparation

RESEARCH & EDUCATION ASSOCIATION
61 Ethel Road W. • Piscataway, New Jersey 08854
Phone: (732) 819-8880   **website: www.rea.com**

Please send me more information about your Test Prep books

Name _____

Address _____

City _____ State _____ Zip _____